STUDY NOTES

ENGLISH LANGUAGE

VOLUME - 2

For All Banking Exams

ENGLISH LANGUAGE

PARA JUMBLES

PARAJUMBLES - CONCEPT, TYPES, AND APPROACH

Tips and Tricks for solving Para jumbles

Paragraph jumble or jumbled paragraph is one of the most important question types in Bank entrance exams. Para jumbles test your understanding of thought flow. In simple words they test are you able to identify a coherently formed paragraph.

Paragraph jumbles come in different sentence lengths.

1. 5 sentence
2. 6 sentence

Since there are 5 questions linked to a single paragraph jumble, solving it is important. These questions can be solved by following specific strategies. So let us understand the strategies and solve some questions.

How We Should Not Solve a Paragraph Jumble

Since there is time constraint, we should NE ER read the sentences again and again without quickly identifying the connections between the sentences. Test setters generally pickup sentences from newspaper articles, books or magazines and hence each sentence has a link to another. Hence it is absolutely necessary to identify the links between sentences.

How Should We Solve The Paragraph Jumble

The proven technique or strategy to solve is to identify the links between the sentences and arrive at a coherent paragraph. To identify the links, we need to identify the key- words. One effective way is to identify MANDATORY PAIRS.

So let us understand what all mandatory pairs are there and how we can identify them.

Important Mandatory Pairs

Pronoun

enerally, the paragraph jumble will mention a noun first and then use pronouns to point at it. So, we need to simply identify those sentence pair that does that.

For instance:

A. He was carrying his jacket and walked with his head thrown back.

B. As Anette neared the lamp, she saw a figure walking slowly.

C. For a while Michael walked on and she followed twenty paces behind.

D. With a mixture of terror and triumph of recognition she slackened her pace.

E. None of these

Since B mentions that Anette saw a figure. So that makes B the first statement. Now read A. It says that HE was carrying his jacket. So that makes BA a mandatory pair. Next is D as she has recognized the figure. And in C the name of the figure is mentioned.

Chronology/ Time reference

Many a times there is a logical/ time bound event chain present in the paragraph jumble. It could be a series of events, steps etc. We can identify the beginning /start of the event and then find the next event and so on.

For instance:

A. Four days later, Oracle announced its own bid for PeopleSoft, and invited the firm's board to a discussion.

B. Furious that his own plans had been endangered, PeopleSoft's boss, Craig Conway, called Oracle's offer —diabolical, and its boss, Larry Ellison, a —sociopath.

C. In early June, PeopleSoft said that it would buy J.D. Edwards, a smaller rival.

D. Moreover, said Mr. Conway, —he could imagine no price nor combination of price and other conditions to recommend accepting the offer.

E. On June 12th, PeopleSoft turned Oracle down.

First sentence is C as it shows the first event in EARLY JUNE, when PeopleSoft announced its plan. Next sentence is A as FOUR DAYS LATER, ORACLE announced ITS OWN plan. B shows that the plan made PeopleSoft boss unhappy. He said something and in next sentence D added by saying MOREO ER. Then on 12th JUNE PeopleSoft turned down the offer.

Another example

A. Then two astronomers the erman, Johannes epler, and the Italian, alileo alilei started publicly to support the Copernican theory, despite the fact that the orbits it predicted did not quite match the ones observed.

B. His idea was that the sun was stationary at the centre and that the earth and the planets move in circular orbits around the sun.

C. A simple model was proposed in 1514 by a Polish priest, Nicholas Copernicus.

D. Nearly a century passed before this idea was taken seriously.

E. None of these

C is the obvious start as it introduces the idea that in 1514, a simple model was suggested. B then explains the idea proposed by Nicholas Copernicus. Then in D —nearly a century passed indicates the time link. A uses then and thus follows D.

Parts of Speech

Parts of speech such as conjunctions, adjectives and pronouns can also be used to identify the links between sentences.

For instance

A. To avoid this, the QWERTY layout put the keys most likely to be hit in rapid succession on opposite sides. This made the keyboard slow, the story goes, but that was the idea.

B. A different layout, which had been patented by August Dvorak in 1936, was shown to be much faster.

C. The QWERTY design (patented by Christopher Sholes in 1868 and sold to Remington in 1873) aimed to solve a mechanical problem of early typewriters.

D. Yet the Dvorak layout has never been widely adopted, even though (with electric typewriters and then PCs) the anti-jamming rationale for QWERTY has been defunct for years.

E. When certain combinations of keys were struck quickly, the type bars often jammed.

C mentions a problem that the qwerty keyboard aimed to solve. E explains the problem in details. A mentions that to avoid THIS i.e. Type bars often jammed . Qwerty provided a SLOW but sure way. B tells that a faster in comparison to QWERTY keyboard was built. D says that YET despite the faster keyboard designed by Dvorak the D ORA keyboard has not been adopted widely.

Obvious Openers

Sometimes you may find that a sentence has no previous link and introduces the idea of the paragraph jumble.

Such sentence can introduce a concept, be a definition, describe an event, state an observation. In short, it will be the Obvious opener of the paragraph.

A good way to find such sentence would be to look at the first letter of the option and read only that sentence to gauge whether the sentence is an obvious opener or not.

For instance

Since then, intelligence tests have been mostly used to separate dull children in school from average or bright children,

A. so that special education can be provided to the dull.

B. In other words, intelligence tests give us a norm for each age.

C. Intelligence is expressed as intelligence quotient, and tests are developed to indicate what an average child of a certain age can do what a 5- year-old can answer, but a 4-year- old cannot, for instance.

D. Binet developed the first set of such tests in the early 1900s to find out which children in school needed special attention.

E. Intelligence can be measured by tests.

Now according to the options, we have 3 sentences that can be obvious opener. As you can see D says SUCH tests. That means either it should define what tests or a statement prior to it should define the tests as we use SUCH when we have mentioned beforehand something about the word. Since D does not mention that, some other statement should and hence D cannot be obvious openers. C looks attractive as an obvious opener as it says the intelligence is expressed as intelligence quotient and tests are developed. Now for one moment let us consider this option. Then what about E, which also introduces the idea that intelligence can be measured by tests. Since it does not have a word such as THUS, HENCE it cannot be conclusion it can be only at the start of the paragraph or not in the paragraph at all. That means E is START of the idea. Hence E is the obvious opener.

Using conjunctions to find links

There are certain words – firstly, secondly, then, however, consequently, on the other hand, etc. – which show how the idea given in the paragraph jumble flows from start to finish. We can identify these words and then look for the sentence that comes before or after these sentences.

Some commonly used linking words we can use are Cause and Effect Words or phrases explicitly indicating that one thing causes another or logically determines another.

For example:

- accordingly
- in order to
- because
- so...that
- consequently
- therefore
- given
- thus
- hence
- when...then
- if...then

Continuing Idea Words:

These words or phrases support a given sentence, idea or example. Sentences containing these words will generally not be the opening sentence. These sentences will follow immediately the sentence supported.

For example:

- furthermore
- additionally
- also
- and
- indeed
- besides
- as well
- too
- likewise
- moreover

Contrast words:

We can also look for words that indicate a contrast between two ideas or statement,

For example:

• although	• nonetheless	• on the contrary	• notwithstanding
• even though	• instead of	• despite	• in spite of
• however	• in contrast	• Nevertheless	• while

For Instance

- When it appeared last April at the Scripps Research Institute in La Jolla, California, scientists thought it had spoiled their experiment.
- Within an hour of its formation, it had commandeered the organic material in a
- thimble-size test tube and started to make copies of itself.
- Yet its behavior was astonishingly lifelike.
- Then the copies made copies.
- But this snippet of synthetic RNA -- one of the master molecules in the nuclei of all cells -- proved unusually talented.
- The molecule was not alive, at least not in any conventional sense.

Explanation:
A cannot be the start point as it uses —it. Since — 'it' is a pronoun, it should point at something. Since A does not tell what —'it' is, A should come after a sentence that defines what —'it' refers to. Same i the case with B. C, D and E use a contrasting word and thus have to be placed after another sentence. That leaves F as the start. F states that the molecule was not alive. C then continues it by contrasting it by stating that —yet its behavior was life like. Now it is clear that we are talking about molecule and thus A will come after A. A states that scientists thought that the molecule had spoiled their experiment. E will come after it as it states —'but' and states that the molecule was talented. B comes after E by describing the talent i.e. making its copies. In D it is written that —'then', which means after the action described in E, copies made copies.

Be the Master of Paragraph Jumbles

The most effective way to solve paragraph jumbles is to be mechanical in finding links or mandatory pairs. You will find that finding links will give you greater accuracy than any other strategy. And remember PRACTICE at least 100 questions to ace paragraph jumbles.

- Follow the general to specific rule, this means that you should move from an introductory sentence to one that gives the details.
- Try to find sentence which introduces a topic or person or idea. This will be the opening sentence.
- You could also try to find the closing sentence; this sentence will generally be a concluding statement.
- It will not introduce a new idea but conclude what has already been mentioned.
- The next trick which is really helpful in solving Para jumbles is to make mandatory pairs.
- Mandatory pairs are sentences which will necessarily come together. The key to solving Para jumble questions is identification of these connected pairs of statements.

For mandatory pair identification, be on the lookout for:

1. Nouns and pronouns reference Nouns or subjects mentioned in a statement can be replaced by

pronoun in the next statement. Be always on the lookout for such pairs.

2. Subject matching two statements based on the subject form a pair.
3. Time sequences in general, if a given set of statements contains reference to time based events, make sure maintain a particular order that is past-present- future or vice-versa.
4. Transition words such as as

• also	• as well as	• besides	• furthermore	• in addition
• likewise	• moreover	• similarly	• consequently	• hence
• for one thing	• above all	• aside from	• besides	• in other words
• instead	• next	• on one hand	• rather	• in conclusion
• meanwhile	• then	• soon	• after all	all in all
• to sum up		• on the other hand		

Types of Parajumble Questions

Para-jumbles broadly fall in three categories. In each category, the jumbled sentences are coded with an alphabet (usually A, B, C and D).

1. 4/5 sentences are given in a random order and you have to unjumble all of them. Toughest of the lot
2. The opening sentence 4/5 sentences are given and you have to rearrange the group of 4/5 sentences, having been given prior knowledge of the thought that starts off the flow of the discussion.
3. 4/5 sentences the closing sentence is given and you need to correctly sequence 4/5 sentences so that they flow into the last sentence.
4. Opening sentence 4/5 Sentences Closing Sentence are given. Easiest of the lot. You know where the story starts and where it ends. You only have to figure out the screenplay in between

The smartest approach

A. The best approach to solving PJ questions is the free fall one. That is, develop a high reading speed and scan all 4-5 sentences. Try to get a feel of what the passage is about.

B. At this point you need to decide whether this particular paragraph is one which you are comfortable with or not.

C. If you decide to go ahead, then scan the answer options. Are they of any help?

If, for example the options are,

a) BDAC b) BCAD c) CABD d) CBDA

Then you know for sure that this paragraph has to start either with B or C. A quick look at B and C wi tell you which one looks like a better opening sentence and already your choices will be halved.

Similarly, with options,

BDCA b) CDBA c) DCAB d) ACDB

Then we know that it has to end with either B or A. So, browse sentences A and B and see if any one of them look like a concluding sentence.

There might be other indicators to keep an eye out for. For example, if three of the five options start with A and the other two with C/B/D there is a good probability that A is the starting sentence.

If, say, a link CB occurs in more than 2 options then it is something worth paying attention to.

Para jumbles strategies to save time and increase accuracy

Strategy 1:

Once upon a time long ago... / ...and they lived happily after Identify the opening/closing sentence using what we discussed above. Either the tone of the paragraph or the option elimination method.

Strategy 2:

Where s the interlock dude? Identify links between two sentences and try to see if that link exists in multiple answer options (a sure way to know that you are on the right track). A combination of 1 and 2 will take you home most of the time.

Strategy 2a:

Make it personal . Look out for personal pronouns (he, she, it, him, her, you, they). Personal pronouns always refer to a person, place or thing.

Therefore, if a sentence has a personal pronoun without mentioning the person, place or object it is referring to, mark it in your head and scan the paragraph for the original per- son, place or object that it refers to.

For example, if you go back to the opening jumbled paragraph of this article, the third sentence starts with it . We now need to figure out what it refers to and the sentence containing the original it will come before this sentence.

Strategy 2b:

Look for Poriborton (Change, in Mamata Banerjee s tongue). Certain words called transition words help the author to shift from one thought flow to another. In other words, they usher in change. Some transition words that appear regularly are --- hence, besides, simultaneously, in conclusion, etc. While you practice PJs whenever you come across a transition word--- note it down. Make a list

Strategy 2c:

Demonstrate Look for demonstrative pronouns --- this, that, these, those, etc. Again, if you look at our opening paragraph, the first line starts with for this --- now we know that we need to figure out wha this refers to and the sentence containing the original this will come before this sentence.

Strategy 3:

Sometimes the events mentioned in the paragraph can be arranged in a chronological or- der making it easy for you to identify the sequence. Example,

A. Alexander Bain, Scottish clockmaker, patented the electric clock.

B. The next development in accuracy occurred after 1656 with the invention of the pendulum clock.

C. Clocks have played an important role in man s history.

D. Spring-driven clocks appeared during the 15th century, although they are often erroneously credited to Nuremberg watchmaker Peter Henlen around 1511.

It is quite obvious by studying the chronology what the sequence should be.

Strategy 4:

The Chota Rajan Approach. Sometimes you will find that for some terms in the paragraph both the full form and the abbreviation have been used. For Example, IMF --- International Monetary Fund, Charles Dickens --- Dickens, Dr Manmohan Singh --- Dr Singh. In these cases where both the full form as well as the abbreviation is present in different sentences, then the sentence containing the full form will obviously come before the sentence containing the abbreviation.

Strategy 5:

What an Idea Sirji If there are two sentences, one containing an idea and another giving examples of the same idea then the sentence containing the idea should come before the sentence containing the examples. But they need not necessarily be exactly side by side.

Example,

A Russia possesses the largest stockpiles of weapons of mass destruction in the world.

B 489 missiles carrying up to 1,788 warheads and 12 submarines carrying up to 609 war- heads form a looming threat.

A will come before B in this case, even though there might be sentences in between.

Strategy 6:

An article of faith. It is highly unlikely that the definite article the will be part of an opening sentence. If a/an and the both are used for the same noun then the sentence containing the will come after the sentence containing a/an.

Myths on Para jumbles

Paragraph jumbles, or as they are fondly called, para jumbles, are sets of connected statements in some random order, which when unjumbled, create a meaningful paragraph. There aren't any straight-forward approaches to solving Para Jumbles. With as many approaches as you can possibly think of, each Para jumble has a unique solution.

There are many myths on Para Jumbles that make them mind-boggling
Myth 1: Para jumbles are the most difficult questions in the English section.
The truth: They really aren't We hope these tips will help you believe it.

Myth 2: Oh, options are the only saving grace
The truth: Para Jumbles can very well be solved without options.

Myth 3: You don't need to be good in vocabulary for Para Jumbles.
The truth: Sorry, vocabulary can actually help go a long way in solving the Para Jumble.

Each Para Jumble can make use of one or more of these tips for solving. Do note that these tips should be applied depending on the unique Para Jumble question posed to you. Some problems can be solved by taking articles as a cue, while some may need pronouns as a guide.

Here are a few tips to successfully solve Para Jumbles:

1. **Look for the sentence that clearly introduces a person, place, committee, or concept in the Para Jumble. That will most likely be the opening sentence.**

Here is an example:

a) He was looking forward to opening up the presents in the solitude of his room.

b) Sanjay's birthday was celebrated with a big bash.

c) But the guests insisted he open them up right there.

d) Several people arrived at his home bearing gifts, both big and small.

e) None of these

Introductory Line:
Clearly the first line must be statement B. This is because the whole passage talks about gifts and guests and what happens at birthdays. So, the first sentence must necessarily introduce the person whose birthday it is. He is referred to by his name in this sentence whereas the remaining sentences refer to him as 'he'. This is another indication that sentence B is the opening line.

Central Theme
Always spot the central theme of each Para Jumble. The flow of the story/dialogue goes a long way in piecing together the paragraph in the correct order.

2. **Follow the activities:**

At times, the Para Jumble will have sentences talking about activities. In such cases by just analyzing which activity happens when, the question can be solved very easily. Take this case for example

a) He accumulates some capital and goes into a business venture with his sons.

b) In order to increase his salary he works through the night.

c) They open shop to create men's garments.

d) Later he takes the garments and sells it on New York streets.

e) He takes garments from the sweatshop to finish at home with the help of his wife and older children at night.

f) A Russian tailor artisan comes to America, takes to the needle trade, works in sweatshop to small salary.

Central theme:

The struggle of a tailor and his steps to success.

Activity Tracking:

Finding the opening sentence here is cakewalk. Sentence F clearly specifies the person and his work, so it's the opening statement. Now a sequence unfolds.

a) A man works in a shop to earn his daily bread. He then goes home and works again with his family's help. He then starts working through the night to earn more. Only after having worked day and night does his work get ready for sale.

b) The sequence just shown should give you hints for part of the answer. After F, the order is E-B-D.

c) Sentence C speaks of a shop that the man opens. So he has to arrange for the capital first. Hence A will come before C.

d) Therefore, the logical order is F-E-B-D-A-C.

If the sentences are too lengthy, do not spend a lot of time reading every detail of it. Be vigilant and quick in spotting 'special words' like connectives, articles, pronouns and adjectives.

3. Connectives:

There will be sentences having connectives like

- although
- though
- if
- until
- since
- but
- then
- after
- alternatively
- besides
- yet
- and
- because
- consequently
- notwithstanding
- when
- for
- meanwhile
- furthermore
- however
- whoever
- therefore
- whatever
- whenever
- nevertheless
- moreover
- whereas

These sentences are almost never the opening ones. They always refer to people or events mentioned in previous sentences.

For example:

1. Friendly wash by many other smaller brands have challenged the giants by offering prices which attracted the value-conscious Indian consumer.
2. **In fact** unbranded players are offering packs which are twice the size of a branded product with similar or better quality at cheaper prices.

Central theme:

- The tough competition given to FMC companies by smaller brands.
- Here the connective 'in fact' clearly indicates that sentence B should follow A. Hence the correct order is A-B.

4. Articles:

- Even articles can help to some extent in these questions.
- 'The' is a definite article, whereas 'a' and 'an' are indefinite articles. 'the' is used to denote something or someone specific or when the person or thing for which the article has been used has already been introduced.
- 'A' or 'an' are used while introducing something for the first time and also for stating general facts. Like, A hit- and-run case usually has a ten year jail term as punishment in India.

For example:

A. **A** boy and his friend played all day in the garden near our house.

B. The next day, I didn't see **the** boy in the garden, though his friend was there.

Central theme:
Boy playing in the garden

In the second sentence, 'the' has been used along with 'boy' because he has already been introduced to the reader in another sentence. Also, here we are talking specifically about that boy. Hence, the correct order is A-B.

5. Pronouns:
Pronouns like he, she, they, it, them, their, him, her etc. are used when the person being talked about has already been introduced. Some Para Jumbles can be tackled by taking pronouns as a guide.

For example:

A. **They** gathered together the death certificates from residents of the town, going back to as many years as they could.

B. **Wolf** decided to investigate.

C. **He** enlisted the support of his students and colleagues from Oklahoma.

Central theme:
An act of investigation

- Since the sentence B clearly states the person, Wolf, it is undoubtedly the opening sentence.
- Next comes sentence C where pronoun 'he' refers to Wolf. It would make no sense if sentence C came before B. Only after Wolf has been introduced, should we use 'he' to refer to Wolf.
- After Wolf has enlisted the support of his friends, we can refer to them as 'they'. So, sentence A is the final one in the passage. Clearly sentence A cannot be used before this because the only one introduced in the first sentence is Wolf and the group of people has only been introduce

in the second sentence. So, we can refer to the group as 'they' only after this second introduction.

- The complete answer is thus B-C-A.

However, in case of pronouns in the first person like 'I', taking cues from them can get baffling. Such Para Jumbles have to be solved using other approaches.

For example:

A. **I** am a student preparing for the SBI PO.

B. **I** request you to provide some helpful tips to solve the logical reasoning questions.

Central theme:
An SBI PO aspirant and his request.

Here, pronouns can be of no help. It is best to think of it this way only after introducing yourself can you talk about your need for some helpful tips. Hence, the order is A-B.

6. **Adjectives:**

Adjectives like 'simpler', 'better', 'cleverer' etc. are comparative. Hence, they always hold a relation to other things. Such adjectives can also be of good help in solving Para Jumbles.

For example:

A. The solution that you had put up was **good.**

B. Riya had posted her solution that I found to be **better.**

Central theme:
Solutions posted by two people.

Here, of course, sentence B has to come after A due to the comparative adjective 'better'.

Para Jumble 1:

1. Post offices and Public sector banks could supplement micro-credit institutions in this regard.
2. They are trusted institutions, and have already built-up credit and savings channels for the poor. In a recent paper, Wouter an inneken of the International Labor Organization has argued that micro-finance institutions could play an important role in providing social security.
3. To overcome this weakness, inneken suggests that micro-credit organizations should out- source the insurance part of their business.
4. But one problem is that most micro-credit institutions are small and lack expertise in the insurance business.

Central theme:
Micro-finance institutions, how they benefit people, problems faced by them and solution to their problems.

- Sentence C should be the opening sentence because it clearly mentions the name of the person, Wouter an inneken and his argument.
- It is essential to note that the Para Jumble is about the institutions, not inneken. Hence, sentence B with pronoun 'they' referring to the institutions should come after C. They go on to give more information about micro-finance institutions.
- Sentences A and D talk about some solutions. So, sentence E which poses the problem should come before them.
- Between A and D, statement D will clearly come first, because it is a suggestion for solving the problem and the method of solving it is in sentence A.
- Therefore the order is C-B-E-D-A.

Para Jumble 2:

1. The former Act imposed severe restrictions on the freedom of the press and the latter forbade the possession of arms by Indians.
2. Many measures of the government provoked widespread agitation.
3. The British government consistently followed a policy of repression after 1857.
4. Two of these were the ernacular Press Act of 1878 and the Arms Act of 1897.

Central theme:

The repressive policy of the British government.

- Sentence C specifies the people (i.e., the British government) and their policy most clearly. Hence it is the opening one.
- Sentence B should follow C as it talks about the measures adopted in the policy.
- Sentence D should follow B as 'these' in D refers to the measures taken by the government which are Draconian Acts.
- Sentence A again talks about the Acts and uses the words 'former' and 'latter'. These words refer to the Acts mentioned in D. Therefore, logically, A will come after D.
- The logical arrangement of the above Para Jumble is C- B-D-A.

Para Jumble 3:

A. Here I would like to echo the words of former President of India, Dr. A.P.J. Abdul alam — A nation's progress depends about how its people think.

B. We have to act with conviction to realize our dream.

C. We Indians have to think as a nation and dream to transform our country into a super power.

D. It is very unfortunate that economically resurgent India still remains home to the world's largest population of poor, hungry and illiterate people.

E. Besides these, rapidly increasing population, rampant corruption, exploitation of women, child labour, communalism are some of the issues which need to be worked upon.

F. Tragically, hunger remains India's biggest lingering problem with an estimated 7000 Indians dying hunger every single day.

. Along with chronic hunger, deep poverty and high illiteracy also continue to blight the lives of millions of our people.

Central theme:

Problems faced by Indians

Locating the opening sentence here is a bit tricky. But on close inspection of some special words, sentence D seems most apt for the opening sentence. That is because of the following

- Sentence A has 'here' implying 'in this situation'.
- Sentences B and C can't be the opening sentence as we don't give solutions before discussing problems.
- Sentence E has the connective 'besides these'.
- Sentences F and give detailed views on hunger and illiteracy as problems in India.
- Sentence D hence should be the opening sentence.
- Notice how the process of elimination has been used to spot the opening sentence.
- Sentences F and should follow next. after F as it has the connective along with 'chronic hunger'.
- Sentence E again with a connective 'besides these' implying besides hunger, poverty and illiteracy should come after .
- Sentence A with 'here' meaning 'in this situation of problems…' should follow E. Also Dr. alam's quote tells that India's progress depends on how its people think.
- Therefore, Sentence C gives the response to A that we have to think as a nation.
- Sentence B, the only one left, is the concluding one. Therefore, the correct order is D-F- -E-A-C-B

REARRANGEMENT OF SENTENCE

Rearrangement of Sentences

Direction: Given below is a set of statements, not necessarily in the correct order. You are required to identify the correct sequence from the options given below and mark that as your answer.

A. To be sure, the growth even in this key area trails the pace of 9.8% that was reported in April 2018 by a wide margin.

B. Hearteningly, capital goods, a sector that serves as a closely tracked proxy for business spending intentions, posted a 2.5% expansion, snapping three straight months of contraction.

C. In fact, manufacturing output growth, which had decelerated sharply from the pace of 8.2% in October to a revised level of less than 0.1% in March, rebounded to a four-month high of 2.8%.

D. A look at the use-based classification reveals that all six segments were in positive territory, with only infrastructure and construction goods marking a slowdown providing cause for some concern.

E. Industrial output rose 3.4% in April, buoyed by a generally broad-based revival that saw electricity, mining and even manufacturing post fast growth.

F. Industrial activity in the new financial year appears to have started on a healthier note than the trend witnessed in the last quarter of the previous fiscal, the government's latest quick estimates show.

1. Which among the following will be the THIRD sentence after the re-arrangement?

A. E B. F C. D D. C E. A

2. Which among the following will be the SIXTH (LAST) sentence after the re-arrangement?

A. D B. C C. A D. B E. F

3. Which among the following will be the SECOND sentence after the re-arrangement?

A. A B. B C. C D. D E. E

4. Which among the following will be the FIFTH sentence after the re-arrangement?

A. B B. C C. D D. F E. A

5. Which among the following will be the FIRST sentence after the re-arrangement?

A. B B. E C. F D. C E. A

Correct Answers:

1	2	3	4	Z5
D	C	E	A	C

Explanations:

1. If we go through the given context we can see that we are talking about the industrial output scenario of the country and the figures that have been published recently by the government in order to support the said growth. The whole passage is regarding the analysis of the figures published based on various industries and specific sectors.

Now, coming to the statements given, we can only start the paragraph with F since it lays out the premise of the context. It makes sense also since it states that the government estimates have shown that the industrial activity has started on a brighter note in this financial year. The succeeding sentences will further analyze the whole thing. This makes F the first sentence.

Connectors:
F and E:
F: Industrial activity in the new financial year appears to have started on a healthier note than the trend witnessed in the last quarter of the previous fiscal, **the government's latest quick estimates show.**

E: **Industrial output rose 3.4% in April,** buoyed by a generally broad-based revival that saw electricity, mining and even manufacturing post fast growth.

E and C:
E: **Industrial output rose** 3.4% in April, **buoyed by a generally broad-based revival** that saw electricity, mining and even manufacturing post fast growth.

C: **In fact, manufacturing output growth**, which had decelerated sharply from the pace of 8.2% in October to a revised level of less than 0.1% in March, **rebounded to a four-month high of 2.8%.**

C and D:
C: **In fact, manufacturing output growth**, which had decelerated sharply from the pace of 8.2% in October to a revised level of less than 0.1% in March, **rebounded to a four-month high of 2.8%.**

D: **A look at the use-based classification reveals that all six segments were in positive territory**, with only infrastructure and construction goods marking a slowdown providing cause for some concern.

D and B:
D: A look at the use-based classification reveals that all six segments were in positive territory, with only infrastructure and construction goods marking a slowdown **providing cause for some concern.**

B: **Hearteningly, capital goods**, a sector that serves as a closely tracked proxy for business spending intentions, **posted a 2.5% expansion**, snapping three straight months of contraction.

B and A:
B: **Hearteningly, capital goods**, a sector that serves as a closely tracked proxy for business spending intentions, **posted a 2.5% expansion, snapping three straight months of contraction.**

A: To be sure, **the growth even in this key area trails** the pace of 9.8% that was reported in April 2018 by a wide margin.
The correct sequence of sentences would be: **FECDBA**
This makes Option D the correct choice among the given options.

2. If we go through the given context we can see that we are talking about the industrial output scenario of the country and the figures that have been published recently by the government in order to support the said growth. The whole passage is regarding the analysis of the figures published based on various industries and specific sectors.

Now, coming to the statements given, we can only start the paragraph with F since it lays out the premise of the context. It makes sense also since it states that the government estimates have shown that the industrial activity has started on a brighter note in this financial year. The succeeding sentences will further analyze the whole thing. This makes F the first sentence.

Connectors:
F and E:
F: Industrial activity in the new financial year appears to have started on a healthier note than the trend witnessed in the last quarter of the previous fiscal, **the government's latest quick estimates show.**

E: **Industrial output rose 3.4% in April,** buoyed by a generally broad-based revival that saw electricity, mining and even manufacturing post fast growth.

E and C:
E: **Industrial output rose** 3.4% in April, **buoyed by a generally broad-based revival** that saw electricity, mining and even manufacturing post fast growth.

C: **In fact, manufacturing output growth**, which had decelerated sharply from the pace of 8.2% in October to a revised level of less than 0.1% in March, **rebounded to a four-month high of 2.8%.**

C and D:
C: **In fact, manufacturing output growth**, which had decelerated sharply from the pace of 8.2% in October to a revised level of less than 0.1% in March, **rebounded to a four-month high of 2.8%.**

D: **A look at the use-based classification reveals that all six segments were in positive territory**, with only infrastructure and construction goods marking a slowdown providing cause for some concern.

D and B:
D: A look at the use-based classification reveals that all six segments were in positive territory, with only infrastructure and construction goods marking a slowdown **providing cause for some concern.**

B: **Hearteningly, capital goods**, a sector that serves as a closely tracked proxy for business spending intentions, **posted a 2.5% expansion**, snapping three straight months of contraction.

B and A:
B: **Hearteningly, capital goods**, a sector that serves as a closely tracked proxy for business spending intentions, **posted a 2.5% expansion, snapping three straight months of contraction.**

A: To be sure, **the growth even in this key area trails** the pace of 9.8% that was reported in April 2018 by a wide margin.

The correct sequence of sentences would be: **FECDBA**
This makes Option C the correct choice among the given options.

3. If we go through the given context we can see that we are talking about the industrial output scenario of the country and the figures that have been published recently by the government in order to support the said growth. The whole passage is regarding the analysis of the figures published based on various industries and specific sectors.

Now, coming to the statements given, we can only start the paragraph with F since it lays out the premise of the context. It makes sense also since it states that the government estimates have shown that the industrial activity has started on a brighter note in this financial year. The succeeding sentences will further analyze the whole thing. This makes F the first sentence.

Connectors:
F and E:
F: Industrial activity in the new financial year appears to have started on a healthier note than the trend witnessed in the last quarter of the previous fiscal, **the government's latest quick estimates show.**

E: **Industrial output rose 3.4% in April,** buoyed by a generally broad-based revival that saw electricity, mining and even manufacturing post fast growth.

E and C:
E: **Industrial output rose** 3.4% in April, **buoyed by a generally broad-based revival** that saw electricity, mining and even manufacturing post fast growth.

C: **In fact, manufacturing output growth**, which had decelerated sharply from the pace of 8.2% in October to a revised level of less than 0.1% in March, **rebounded to a four-month high of 2.8%.**

C and D:
C: **In fact, manufacturing output growth**, which had decelerated sharply from the pace of 8.2% in October to a revised level of less than 0.1% in March, **rebounded to a four-month high of 2.8%.**

D: **A look at the use-based classification reveals that all six segments were in positive territory**, with only infrastructure and construction goods marking a slowdown providing cause for some concern.

D and B:
D: A look at the use-based classification reveals that all six segments were in positive territory, with only infrastructure and construction goods marking a slowdown **providing cause for some concern.**

B: **Hearteningly, capital goods**, a sector that serves as a closely tracked proxy for business spending intentions, **posted a 2.5% expansion**, snapping three straight months of contraction.

B and A:
B: **Hearteningly, capital goods**, a sector that serves as a closely tracked proxy for business spending intentions, **posted a 2.5% expansion, snapping three straight months of contraction.**

A: To be sure, **the growth even in this key area trails** the pace of 9.8% that was reported in April 2018 by a wide margin.

The correct sequence of sentences would be: **FECDBA**
This makes Option E the correct choice among the given options.

4. If we go through the given context we can see that we are talking about the industrial output scenario of the country and the figures that have been published recently by the government in order to support the said growth. The whole passage is regarding the analysis of the figures published based on various industries and specific sectors.

Now, coming to the statements given, we can only start the paragraph with F since it lays out the premise of the context. It makes sense also since it states that the government estimates have shown that the industrial activity has started on a brighter note in this financial year. The succeeding sentences will further analyze the whole thing. This makes F the first sentence.

Connectors:
F and E:
F: Industrial activity in the new financial year appears to have started on a healthier note than the trend witnessed in the last quarter of the previous fiscal, **the government's latest quick estimates show.**

E: **Industrial output rose 3.4% in April,** buoyed by a generally broad-based revival that saw electricity, mining and even manufacturing post fast growth.

E and C:
E: **Industrial output rose** 3.4% in April, **buoyed by a generally broad-based revival** that saw electricity, mining and even manufacturing post fast growth.

C: **In fact, manufacturing output growth**, which had decelerated sharply from the pace of 8.2% in October to a revised level of less than 0.1% in March, **rebounded to a four-month high of 2.8%.**

C and D:
C: **In fact, manufacturing output growth**, which had decelerated sharply from the pace of 8.2% in October to a revised level of less than 0.1% in March, **rebounded to a four-month high of 2.8%.**

D: **A look at the use-based classification reveals that all six segments were in positive territory**, with only infrastructure and construction goods marking a slowdown providing cause for some concern.

D and B:
D: A look at the use-based classification reveals that all six segments were in positive territory, with only infrastructure and construction goods marking a slowdown **providing cause for some concern.**

B: **Hearteningly, capital goods**, a sector that serves as a closely tracked proxy for business spending intentions, **posted a 2.5% expansion**, snapping three straight months of contraction.

B and A:
B: **Hearteningly, capital goods**, a sector that serves as a closely tracked proxy for business spending intentions, **posted a 2.5% expansion, snapping three straight months of contraction.**

A: To be sure, **the growth even in this key area trails** the pace of 9.8% that was reported in April 2018 by a wide margin.

The correct sequence of sentences would be: **FECDBA**
This makes Option A the correct choice among the given options.

5. If we go through the given context we can see that we are talking about the industrial output scenario of the country and the figures that have been published recently by the government in order to support the said growth. The whole passage is regarding the analysis of the figures published based on various industries and specific sectors.

Now, coming to the statements given, we can only start the paragraph with F since it lays out the premise of the context. It makes sense also since it states that the government estimates have shown that the industrial activity has started on a brighter note in this financial year. The succeeding sentences will further analyze the whole thing. This makes F the first sentence.

Connectors:

F and E:
F: Industrial activity in the new financial year appears to have started on a healthier note than the trend witnessed in the last quarter of the previous fiscal, **the government's latest quick estimates show.**

E: **Industrial output rose 3.4% in April,** buoyed by a generally broad-based revival that saw electricity, mining and even manufacturing post fast growth.

E and C:
E: **Industrial output rose** 3.4% in April, **buoyed by a generally broad-based revival** that saw electricity, mining and even manufacturing post fast growth.

C: **In fact, manufacturing output growth**, which had decelerated sharply from the pace of 8.2% in October to a revised level of less than 0.1% in March, **rebounded to a four-month high of 2.8%.**

C and D:
C: **In fact, manufacturing output growth**, which had decelerated sharply from the pace of 8.2% in October to a revised level of less than 0.1% in March, **rebounded to a four-month high of 2.8%.**

D: **A look at the use-based classification reveals that all six segments were in positive territory**, with only infrastructure and construction goods marking a slowdown providing cause for some concern.

D and B:
D: A look at the use-based classification reveals that all six segments were in positive territory, with only infrastructure and construction goods marking a slowdown **providing cause for some concern.**

B: **Hearteningly, capital goods**, a sector that serves as a closely tracked proxy for business spending intentions, **posted a 2.5% expansion**, snapping three straight months of contraction.

B and A:
B: **Hearteningly, capital goods**, a sector that serves as a closely tracked proxy for business spending intentions, **posted a 2.5% expansion, snapping three straight months of contraction.**

A: To be sure, **the growth even in this key area trails** the pace of 9.8% that was reported in April 2018 by a wide margin.

The correct sequence of sentences would be: **FECDBA**

Direction: In each of the questions given below, a set of six sentences is given, which are jumbled in any random order. Rearrange the sentences in the right order and answer the questions that follow.

A. In that mood of nostalgia, ancient poets—Homer and Aeschylus, in particular—started getting described as vates or prophets, and language—more particularly, "the original" language—as a spiritually potent agency of human liberation.

B. The idea that a nation should ideally have a single language that will keep the people bound together was added to its range of signification during the early 19th century.

C. This was the time when a new kind of longing for the past was emerging among the English painters and poets as a result of the devastation of the countryside due to rapid industrialisation.

D. In its semantic trajectory within the English language, "nation" was initially rooted in the idea of "belonging to a geographical area or location."

E. It decidedly referred to an area, territory and the people who inhabited it.

F. The term "nation" was drawn by the English language, during its historical phase known as Middle English, from the Latin root nationem signifying birth and ancestry.

1. **Which among the following will come after the FOURTH sentence after the rearrangement?**

A. F B. E C. C D. B E. None of the above

2. **Which among the following would be the FIRST sentence of the paragraph after the rearrangement?**

A. D B. F C. E D. C E. None of the above

3. **Which among the following would be the LAST sentence of the paragraph after the rearrangement?**

A. C B. B C. E D. D E. A

4. Which among the following would come immediately after the SECOND sentence of the paragraph after the rearrangement?

A. F　　B. B　　C. C　　D. E　　E. None of the above

5. Which among the following would be the SECOND sentence of the paragraph after the rearrangement?

A. E　　B. F　　C. A　　D. C　　E. D

Correct Answers:

1	2	3	4	5
C	B	E	D	E

Explanations :

1. The given passage is regarding the way in which we are trying to understand the concept of nation starting from the source of the word. It explains in detail how the concept is used in the notional term and also generally. Now coming to the given sentences we can see that only the Statement F is the first sentence of the passage as it gives us the premise based on which we can say that the passage is regarding the concept of nation.

Connectors:
F and D:

F: The term "nation" was drawn by the English language, during its historical phase known as Middle English, from the Latin root nationem signifying birth and ancestry.

D: In its semantic trajectory within the English language, "nation" was initially rooted in the idea of "belonging to a geographical area or location."

D and E:

D: In its semantic trajectory within the English language, "nation" was initially rooted in the idea of "belonging to a geographical area or location."

E: It decidedly referred to an area, territory and the people who inhabited it.

E and B:

E: It decidedly referred to an area, territory and the people who inhabited it.

B: The idea that a nation should ideally have a single language that will keep the people bound together was added to its range of signification during the early 19th century.

B and C:

B: The idea that a nation should ideally have a single language that will keep the people bound together was added to its range of signification during the early 19th century.

C: This was the time when a new kind of longing for the past was emerging among the English painters and poets as a result of the devastation of the countryside due to rapid industrialisation.

C and A:

C: This was the time when a new kind of longing for the past was emerging among the English painters and poets as a result of the devastation of the countryside due to rapid industrialisation.

A: In that mood of nostalgia, ancient poets—Homer and Aeschylus, in particular—started getting described as vates or prophets, and language—more particularly, "the original" language—as a spiritually potent agency of human liberation.

The correct sequence of sentences would be: **FDEBCA**

This makes Option C the correct choice among the given options.

2. The given passage is regarding the way in which we are trying to understand the concept of nation starting from the source of the word. It explains in detail how the concept is used in the notional term and also generally. Now coming to the given sentences we can see that only the Statement F is the first sentence of the passage as it gives us the premise based on which we can say that the passage is regarding the concept of nation.

Connectors:
F and D:

F: The term "nation" was drawn by the English language, during its historical phase known as Middle English, from the Latin root nationem signifying birth and ancestry.

D: In its semantic trajectory within the English language, "nation" was initially rooted in the idea of "belonging to a geographical area or location."

D and E:

D: In its semantic trajectory within the English language, "nation" was initially rooted in the idea of "belonging to a geographical area or location."

E: It decidedly referred to an area, territory and the people who inhabited it.

E and B:

E: It decidedly referred to an area, territory and the people who inhabited it.

B: The idea that a nation should ideally have a single language that will keep the people bound together was added to its range of signification during the early 19th century.

B and C:

B: The idea that a nation should ideally have a single language that will keep the people bound together was added to its range of signification during the early 19th century.

C: This was the time when a new kind of longing for the past was emerging among the English painters and poets as a result of the devastation of the countryside due to rapid industrialisation.

C and A:

C: This was the time when a new kind of longing for the past was emerging among the English painters and poets as a result of the devastation of the countryside due to rapid industrialisation.

A: In that mood of nostalgia, ancient poets—Homer and Aeschylus, in particular—started getting described as vates or prophets, and language—more particularly, "the original" language—as a spiritually potent agency of human liberation.

The correct sequence of sentences would be: **FDEBCA**

This makes Option B the correct choice among the given options.

3. The given passage is regarding the way in which we are trying to understand the concept of nation starting from the source of the word. It explains in detail how the concept is used in the notional term and also generally. Now coming to the given sentences we can see that only the Statement F is the first sentence of the passage as it gives us the premise based on which we can say that the passage is regarding the concept of nation.

Connectors:
F and D:

F: The term "nation" was drawn by the English language, during its historical phase known as Middle English, from the Latin root nationem signifying birth and ancestry.

D: In its semantic trajectory within the English language, "nation" was initially rooted in the idea of "belonging to a geographical area or location."

D and E:

D: In its semantic trajectory within the English language, "nation" was initially rooted in the idea of "belonging to a geographical area or location."
E: It decidedly referred to an area, territory and the people who inhabited it.

E and B:

E: It decidedly referred to an area, territory and the people who inhabited it.

B: The idea that a nation should ideally have a single language that will keep the people bound together was added to its range of signification during the early 19th century.

B and C:

B: The idea that a nation should ideally have a single language that will keep the people bound together was added to its range of signification during the early 19th century.
C: This was the time when a new kind of longing for the past was emerging among the English painters and poets as a result of the devastation of the countryside due to rapid industrialisation.

C and A:

C: This was the time when a new kind of longing for the past was emerging among the English painters and poets as a result of the devastation of the countryside due to rapid industrialisation.

A: In that mood of nostalgia, ancient poets—Homer and Aeschylus, in particular—started getting described as vates or prophets, and language—more particularly, "the original" language—as a spiritually potent agency of human liberation.

The correct sequence of sentences would be: **FDEBCA**

This makes Option E the correct choice among the given options.

4. The given passage is regarding the way in which we are trying to understand the concept of nation starting from the source of the word. It explains in detail how the concept is used in the notional term and also generally. Now coming to the given sentences we can see that only the Statement F is the first sentence of the passage as it gives us the premise based on which we can say that the passage is regarding the concept of nation.

Connectors:
F and D:

F: The term "nation" was drawn by the English language, during its historical phase known as Middle English, from the Latin root nationem signifying birth and ancestry.

D: In its semantic trajectory within the English language, "nation" was initially rooted in the idea of "belonging to a geographical area or location."

D and E:

D: In its semantic trajectory within the English language, "nation" was initially rooted in the idea of "belonging to a geographical area or location."
E: It decidedly referred to an area, territory and the people who inhabited it.

E and B:

E: It decidedly referred to an area, territory and the people who inhabited it.

B: The idea that a nation should ideally have a single language that will keep the people bound together was added to its range of signification during the early 19th century.

B and C:
B: The idea that a nation should ideally have a single language that will keep the people bound together was added to its range of signification during the early 19th century.
C: This was the time when a new kind of longing for the past was emerging among the English painters and poets as a result of the devastation of the countryside due to rapid industrialisation.

C and A:

C: This was the time when a new kind of longing for the past was emerging among the English painters and poets as a result of the devastation of the countryside due to rapid industrialisation.

A: In that mood of nostalgia, ancient poets—Homer and Aeschylus, in particular—started getting described as vates or prophets, and language—more particularly, "the original" language—as a spiritually potent agency of human liberation.

The correct sequence of sentences would be: **FDEBCA**

This makes Option D the correct choice among the given options.

5. The given passage is regarding the way in which we are trying to understand the concept of nation starting from the source of the word. It explains in detail how the concept is used in the notional term and also generally. Now coming to the given sentences we can see that only the Statement F is the first sentence of the passage as it gives us the premise based on which we can say that the passage is regarding the concept of nation.

Connectors:
F and D:

F: The term "nation" was drawn by the English language, during its historical phase known as Middle English, from the Latin root nationem signifying birth and ancestry.

D: In its semantic trajectory within the English language, "nation" was initially rooted in the idea of "belonging to a geographical area or location."

D and E:

D: In its semantic trajectory within the English language, "nation" was initially rooted in the idea of "belonging to a geographical area or location."
E: It decidedly referred to an area, territory and the people who inhabited it.

E and B:

E: It decidedly referred to an area, territory and the people who inhabited it.

B: The idea that a nation should ideally have a single language that will keep the people bound together was added to its range of signification during the early 19th century.

B and C:

B: The idea that a nation should ideally have a single language that will keep the people bound together was added to its range of signification during the early 19th century.
C: This was the time when a new kind of longing for the past was emerging among the English painters and poets as a result of the devastation of the countryside due to rapid industrialisation.

C and A:

C: This was the time when a new kind of longing for the past was emerging among the English painters and poets as a result of the devastation of the countryside due to rapid industrialisation.

A: In that mood of nostalgia, ancient poets—Homer and Aeschylus, in particular—started getting described as vates or prophets, and language—more particularly, "the original" language—as a spiritually potent agency of human liberation.

The correct sequence of sentences would be: **FDEBCA**

This makes Option E the correct choice among the given options.

Directions: Rearrange the following six sentences (A), (B), (C), (D), (E) and (F) in a proper sequence to form a meaningful paragraph. Then answer the questions given below.

A. They took to social media to criticize the university administration.

B. But the decision did not go well with the students.

C. Recently, XYZ University decided to install suicide prevention devices on hostel fans after a spree of three suicides in hostel rooms in the last one year.

D. Incidents of students committing suicides are on the rise in India.

E. When contacted, the VC of the university said that a proper grievance redressal mechanism would be set up soon.

F. They wanted the administration to employ a mechanism to check discrimination and harassment on campus.

1. Which of the following should be the SECOND statement after rearrangement?

A. A B. B C. C D. F E. E

2. Which of the following should be the FOURTH statement after rearrangement?

A. A B. B C. C D. D E. F

3. Which of the following should be the THIRD statement after rearrangement?

A. A B. B C. F D. D E. E

4. Which of the following should be the FIRST statement after rearrangement?

A. A B. B C. C D. D E. E

5. Which of the following should be the SIXTH statement after rearrangement?

A. A B. B C. C D. D E. E

Correct Answers:

1	2	3	4	5
C	A	B	D	E

Common explanations:

Analysing the given sentences, we see that, sentence B starts with the conjunction 'but'.

But, the beginning sentence cannot begin with a conjunction. Hence, it can be discarded as the beginning sentence.

Sentence A and sentence F start with the pronoun 'they'. They cannot also be the beginning sentences.

Sentence E, beginning with 'when', does not introduce the idea flowing through the sentences.

Between sentence C and sentence D, sentence D introduces the idea of the entire paragraph. Hence, it will be the beginning sentence.

Connecting D and C:-

Incidents of **students committing suicides** are on the rise in India.

Recently, XYZ University decided to install suicide prevention devices on hostel fans after **a spree of three suicides in hostel rooms in the last one year**.

Sentence C elaborates upon the idea introduced through sentence D. Sentence D and sentence C form a mandatory pair. **[D-C]**

Connecting C and B:-

Recently, **XYZ University decided to install suicide prevention devices on hostel fans** after a spree of three suicides in hostel rooms in the last one year.

But the decision did not go well with the students.

Sentence B gives more information about the aftermath of the decision taken by the university. Sentence B closely follows the idea presented through sentence C. **[C-B]**

Connecting B and A:-

But the decision **did not go well with the students**.

They took to social media to criticize the university administration.

Sentence A tells us how the students gave vent to their displeasure (=We came to know of this displeasure in sentence B). Sentence A tells us that the students took to social media to criticize the administration of the university. "They" of sentence A is the substitute of "the students" of sentence B. **[B-A]**

Connecting A and F:-

They took to social media to criticize the university administration.

They wanted the administration to employ a mechanism to check discrimination and harassment on campus.

Sentence F presents the demands of the students and closely follows sentence A. **[A-F]**

Connecting F and E:-

They wanted the administration to employ **a mechanism to check discrimination and harassment on campus**.

When contacted, the VC of the university said that **a proper grievance redressal mechanism would be set up soon**.

Sentence E tells us about the university administration's stance with respect to the students' demands (that was presented through sentence F). **[F-E]**

The correct sequence is: **DCBAFE**

Answers :

1. As per the question, the SECOND statement is C.

   Hence, option C is correct.

2. As per the question, the FOURTH statement is A.

   Hence, option A is correct.

3. As per the question, the THIRD statement is B.

   Hence, option B is correct.

4. As per the question, the FIRST statement is D.

   Hence, option D is correct.

5. As per the question, the SIXTH statement is E.

   Hence, option E is correct.

Directions: Rearrange the following six sentences A, B, C, D, E and F in the proper sequence to form a meaningful paragraph and then answer the question given beside.

A. Last month, the FCA issued a proposal to relax listing conditions for state-owned issuers wishing to qualify for the London Stock Exchange (LSE) Premium Listing Segment – the exchange's "gold standard" segment, governed by stringent regulations.

B. In its consultation paper, the FCA states that "sovereign owners tend to be different from private-sector individuals or entities both in their motivations and in their nature."

C. It is a valid assumption – and precisely the reason why SOEs should not be given preferential regulatory treatment.

D. Amid intense competition for the anticipated listing of Saudi Aramco – the world's largest oil company, owned by the Saudi state – stock exchanges and financial-market regulators are under pressure to provide incentives for the company to dual-list its shares abroad.

E. The proposal is presented as a mere technicality, but it is significant for reasons that extend beyond Saudi Aramco. In fact, it implies that regulators now believe that state-owned enterprises (SOEs) deserve special regulatory treatment.

F. The United Kingdom's Financial Conduct Authority (FCA) seems to be bowing to that pressure.

1. Which of the following would be the THIRD sentence after rearrangement?

A. D | B. C | C. A | D. E | E. B

2. Which of the following would be the LAST (SIXTH) sentence after rearrangement?

A. C | B. D | C. F | D. A | E. B

3. Which of the following would be the FIRST sentence after rearrangement?

A. A | B. B | C. C | D. D | E. F

4. Which of the following would be the FIFTH sentence after rearrangement?

A. E | B. B | C. C | D. D | E. F

5. Which of the following would be the SECOND sentence after rearrangement?

A. E | B. C | C. B | D. D | E. F

Correct Answers:

1	2	3	4	5
C	A	D	B	E

Common explanations :

The subject that is being discussed in the passage is the listing of Saudi Aramco and the role of United Kingdom's Financial Conduct Authority (FCA).

While solving jumbled sentences puzzle, we understand that the statement which gives an overview and not some specific information comes in the beginning in a passage. Therefore sentence "D", which mentions the anticipated listing of the Saudi Aramco, will be the first. Sentence "D" mentions that the stock exchanges are in pressure; while sentence "F" mentions that the Financial Conduct Authority is bowing to that pressure. Therefore Sentence "F" follows sentence "D".

Linking "F" to "A"

The topic of public listing of Saudi Aramco's is mentioned in sentence "D". Sentence "A" explains this topic further by talking about a proposal for listing on the London Stock Exchange.

Linking "A" to "E"

The mention of a proposal in sentence "A" is continued in sentence "E".

Linking "E" to "B"

Sentence "E" mentions that state-owned enterprises (SOEs) deserve special regulatory treatment. State-owned enterprises are also controlled by the sovereign nation.

Sentence "B" also mentions sovereign owners (...that sovereign owners tend to be different from private-sector individuals...). Thus, E must be followed by B.

Linking "B" to "C"

Sentence "B" says - sovereign owners tend to be different from private-sector individuals. Here the phrase "tend" is used to describe an assumption about sovereign owners by FCA.

Sentence "C" mentions assumption in it, therefore, "B" must be followed by "C".

The correct sequence is DFAEBC.

Answers :

1. By following the final sequence which is DFAEBC, we can say that the third sentence is A.

   Hence, the correct answer is option C.

2. By following the final sequence which is DFAEBC, we can say that the last sentence is C.

   Hence, the correct answer is option A.

3. By following the final sequence which is DFAEBC, we can say that the first sentence is A.

   Hence, the correct answer is option D.

4. By following the final sequence which is DFAEBC, we can say that the fifth sentence is B.

   Hence, the correct answer is option B.

5. By following the final sequence which is DFAEBC, we can say that the second sentence is A.

   Hence, the correct answer is option E.

Direction: Given sentences are not in their exact position. Rearrange them to make a coherent paragraph and then answer the questions given below.

A. We do need to guard against unfair trade practices, such as goods made in China being routed through some countries with which India has an FTA, flouting all rules of origin and local value-addition norms.

B. This is integral to the ongoing process of eliminating from Indian business assorted means of enrichment that have little do with efficient creation of value.

C. India can hope to end its present exclusion from global value chains — across various industry segments — through membership of RCEP.

D. At the same time, the government needs to appreciate that global trade and exposure to import competition constitute a sure method of raising Indian industry's competitiveness.

E. In parallel, there's the need to put in place clear-cut safeguards measures to prevent dumping of goods, especially from China.

1. Which of the following should be the FOURTH sentence after the rearrangement?

A. A B. B C. C D. D E. E

2. Which of the following should be the SECOND sentence after the rearrangement?

A. A B. B C. C D. D E. E

3. Which of the following should be the THIRD sentence after the rearrangement?

A. A B. B C. C D. D E. E

4. Which of the following should be the FIRST sentence after the rearrangement?

A. A B. B C. C D. D E. E

5. Which of the following should be the FIFTH sentence after the rearrangement?

A. A B. B C. C D. D E. E

Explanations :

1. The first sentence should seem like an introduction to the topic. After reading all the sentences, statement C seems to be the most appropriate choice. It speaks about India's hope to end its present exclusion from global value chains.

Further, statement E picks up where fragment C has left off and they make sense together. The sentence starts with 'in parallel' which indicates other measures that are to be taken to make India's hopes come true. **Thus, fragment C and fragment E make a pair.**

Now, if we read the sentences carefully, we find that statement E mentions 'dumping of goods' from China and statement A carries on with the mention of 'unfair trade practices' and how goods made in China are routed. They make a meaningful sentence together. **Thus, fragment E and fragment A also make a mandatory pair.** So far, the correct sequence of statements is: **CEA**

The fourth sentence should add meaning to the idea being formed. A complete ban on Chinese goods would be impractical and the government should also consider imports to be an essential part of India's trade competitiveness. Hence, the correct sequence of statements is: **CEADB**

Option D is hence the correct answer.

2. The first sentence should seem like an introduction to the topic. After reading all the sentences, statement C seems to be the most appropriate choice. It speaks about India's hope to end its present exclusion from global value chains.

Further, statement E picks up where fragment C has left off and they make sense together. The sentence starts with 'in parallel' which indicates other measures that are to be taken to make India's hopes come true. **Thus, fragment C and fragment E make a pair.**

Now, if we read the sentences carefully, we find that statement E mentions 'dumping of goods' from China and statement A carries on with the mention of 'unfair trade practices' and how goods made in China are routed. They make a meaningful sentence together. **Thus, fragment E and fragment A also make a mandatory pair.** So far, the correct sequence of statements is: **CEA**

The fourth sentence should add meaning to the idea being formed. A complete ban on Chinese goods would be impractical and the government should also consider imports to be an essential part of India's trade competitiveness. Hence, the correct sequence of statements is: **CEADB**

Option E is hence the correct answer.

3. The first sentence should seem like an introduction to the topic. After reading all the sentences, statement C seems to be the most appropriate choice. It speaks about India's hope to end its present exclusion from global value chains.

Further, statement E picks up where fragment C has left off and they make sense together. The sentence starts with 'in parallel' which indicates other measures that are to be taken to make India's hopes come true. **Thus, fragment C and fragment E make a pair.**

Now, if we read the sentences carefully, we find that statement E mentions 'dumping of goods' from China and statement A carries on with the mention of 'unfair trade practices' and how goods made in China are routed. They make a meaningful sentence together. **Thus, fragment E and fragment A also make a mandatory pair.** So far, the correct sequence of statements is: **CEA**

The fourth sentence should add meaning to the idea being formed. A complete ban on Chinese goods would be impractical and the government should also consider imports to be an essential part of India's trade competitiveness. Hence, the correct sequence of statements is: **CEADB**

Option A is hence the correct answer.

4. The first sentence should seem like an introduction to the topic. After reading all the sentences, statement C seems to be the most appropriate choice. It speaks about India's hope to end its present exclusion from global value chains.

Further, statement E picks up where fragment C has left off and they make sense together. The sentence starts with 'in parallel' which indicates other measures that are to be taken to make India's hopes come true. **Thus, fragment C and fragment E make a pair.**

Now, if we read the sentences carefully, we find that statement E mentions 'dumping of goods' from China and statement A carries on with the mention of 'unfair trade practices' and how goods made in China are routed. They make a meaningful sentence together. **Thus, fragment E and fragment A also make a mandatory pair.** So far, the correct sequence of statements is: **CEA**

The fourth sentence should add meaning to the idea being formed. A complete ban on Chinese goods would be impractical and the government should also consider imports to be an essential part of India's trade competitiveness. Hence, the correct sequence of statements is: **CEADB**

Option C is hence the correct answer.

5. The first sentence should seem like an introduction to the topic. After reading all the sentences, statement C seems to be the most appropriate choice. It speaks about India's hope to end its present exclusion from global value chains.

Further, statement E picks up where fragment C has left off and they make sense together. The sentence starts with 'in parallel' which indicates other measures that are to be taken to make India's hopes come true. **Thus, fragment C and fragment E make a pair.**

Now, if we read the sentences carefully, we find that statement E mentions 'dumping of goods' from China and statement A carries on with the mention of 'unfair trade practices' and how goods made in China are routed. They make a meaningful sentence together. **Thus, fragment E and fragment A also make a mandatory pair.** So far, the correct sequence of statements is: **CEA**

The fourth sentence should add meaning to the idea being formed. A complete ban on Chinese goods would be impractical and the government should also consider imports to be an essential part of India's trade competitiveness. Hence, the correct sequence of statements is: **CEADB**

Option B is hence the correct answer.

SENTENCE CONNECTOR

SENTENCE CONNECTORS

Let us first understand what exactly are Sentence Connectors?

- Another terminology for Sentence Connectors is "synthesis".
- In such type of questions, we are provided with three phrases/connectors. Among these, we need to find out the correct option which when used in the beginning of the sentence will help combine the two statements in a coherent manner.
- We need to bear in mind that after using these connectors to connect these statements, the newly formed sentence should imply the same meaning as expressed in the statement sentences.
- These questions appear somewhat difficult, but are very easy to tackle after some practice and can help you score good marks in the exam.
- The need to join sentences stems from the fact that it will help avoid the monotony that may result due to the use of brief sentences. Hence, to combine them and give them rhythm and style of various lengths and structures, we use sentence connectors.
- Sentence Connectors are words and phrases that are used for the synthesis of sentences, i.e., connect two sentences into one sentence with coherence. "Coherence" means "the quality of being logical and consistent".
- Hence, the correct sentence connector is one that maintains coherence in the given two statements.
- Sentence connectors are used to provide coherence to the statement or paragraphs by presenting a contrast, similarity, consequence, sequence, example, emphasis, dismissal, etc.
- Some important sentence connectors can also be learned by a mnemonic device i.e., "ON A WHITE BUS" is given below.
- The letters of this mnemonic stand for subordinating conjunctions of the English Language:

  O: only if, once
  N: now that
  A: after, although, as
  WH: where, wherever, when, whenever, whether, while
  H: how
  I: in case, if, in order that
  T: though, that
  E: even though, even if
  B: before, because
  U: until, unless
  S: since, so that

Apart from them, there are other ways too to connect simple, complex and compound sentences. They can also be joined by the use of participle, punctuation, initiative, adjective clause, adverbial phrase, adverbial clause, etc. We will try to understand a few of these techniques.

Example 1:
1. We should move away from here.
2. The storm is approaching.

(i) Considering that
(ii) Although we should
(iii) As the storm

1. Only (i)
2. Only (ii)
3. Only (iii)
4. Both (i) and (ii)
5. Both (i) and (iii)

Explanation:
In the first statement, it has been stated that "the storm is approaching". Hence, it is an alarming situation for someone present over there. The second statement states an action that should be taken considering the above problem. The _rst option, "considering that" gives coherence to the two statements if combined - "Considering that the storm is approaching, we should move away from here". "Considering that" is used to indicate that one is thinking about a particular fact/problem/situation when making a judgment or decision.

The second option "although we should" states a contrast and when added to the beginning of any of the given two statements it does not make sense. For example, "Although the storm is approaching, we should move away from here." This statement is not logical. The key to solving questions based on sentence connectors lies in making the statements logical and consistent.

The third option "As the storm" consists of "as". We use "as" in the beginning of a sentence to "state the reason for something". Hence, in the given statement, it is stating the reason to leave a particular place due to imminent danger.

Example 2:
1. They were afraid.
2. The cat would eat them up.

(i) that anytime
(ii) as a matter of fact
(iii) knowing that

Explanation:
These two sentences can be combined in many ways. By using option (i), "They were afraid that anytime the cat would eat them up." It can also be combined by using option (iii), They

were afraid, knowing that the cat would eat them up. Option (ii) is incorrect for combining these sentences because "as a matter of fact" is used to emphasis sentences.

Example 3:
1. The love and adulation he amasses only continues to grow with each passing day.
2. It has been about four years that Sachin retired.

(i) As it
(ii) All in all
(iii) Although

1. Only (i)
2. Only (ii)
3. Only (iii)
4. Both (i) and (ii)
5. Both (i) and (iii)

Explanation:
The given two statements present a contrasting fact that despite the retirement of Sachin about four years ago, his popularity has been growing as the time passes. Now option (i) does not give coherence to the statements. "As" in the beginning of the sentence is used to state a reason.

In the second option, "all in all" is used to state consideration of all aspects of something together.

The third option, "although" is the correct connector to be used. "Although" means "in spite of the fact that". Hence, the correct answer should be option C.

Example 4:
1. She knows nothing about him.
2. He is young and handsome.

(i) Although he is
(ii) Except that
(iii) However, she knows

1. Only (i)
2. Only (ii)
3. Only (iii)
4. Both (i) and (ii)
5. Both (i) and (iii)

Explanation:
In the above-given statements, two different statements are given in which the first one states that the lady knows nothing about a particular person whereas a fact about that

person is mentioned. The given statements can be used by using "except that"- "She knows nothing about him except that he is young and handsome".

Example 5:

1. He keeps his pistol in a holster.
2. This is the holster.

(i) along with his
(ii) in fact
(iii) where he keeps

1. Only (i)
2. Only (ii)
3. Only (iii)
4. Both (i) and (ii)
5. Both (i) and (iii)

Explanation:

In the above-mentioned statements, one statement states information and the other statement provides a brief description. Such types of sentences can be added by the use of "adjective clauses". These two statements can be added in the given way – This is the holster where he keeps his pistol.

Hence, after careful scrutiny of the given statements and understanding their implied meaning you can use appropriate sentence connectors from the given options. A little practice will immensely help you in making you comfortable in identifying the conveyed meaning of the statements and enable you to use appropriate sentence connectors to combine the sentences.

Directions: **You are required to match statements from columns 1 and 2 and find which of the following pairs of statement make sense meaningfully and grammatically.**

Question 1:

Column (1)		Column (2)	
(A)	The eagle was afraid to fly into the sky	(D)	in spite of the Internet has a plethora of options.
(B)	The shrewd businessman quickly	(E)	after remain in captivity for two years.
(C)	Freelancing has always been a popular way to earn money online	(F)	grabbed beneath the opportunity and earned a huge pile of money.

A. Only A-E and C-D
B. Only B-F and C-D
C. Only A-E and B-F
D. Only C-D
E. None of these

Answer: E

Explanation:

Checking A-E:

The eagle was afraid to fly into the sky after remain in captivity for two years. The above sentence is grammatically erroneous. The usage of 'remain' is incorrect. It should have been 'remaining' instead of 'remain'. Hence, the pair A-E is invalid.

Checking B-F:

The shrewd businessman quickly grabbed beneath the opportunity and earned a huge pile of money.
The above sentence is grammatically erroneous. The correct preposition after 'grabbed' would be 'onto'. Hence, the pair B-F is invalid.

Checking C-D:

Freelancing has always been a popular way to earn money online in spite of the Internet has a plethora of options.

The above sentence is grammatically erroneous. The usage of 'in spite of' in the above sentence is incorrect. The correct word in front of 'the internet' would be 'and' instead of the expression 'in spite of'. Hence, the pair C-D is invalid.

Hence, option E is the correct answer.

Question 2:

Column (1)		Column (2)	
(A)	The audience gave the veteran musician	(D)	in the country today and covers over 50 per cent of Kerala households.
(B)	Kudumbashree is one of the largest women- empowerment projects	(E)	a standing ovation.
(C)	Children who have been victims of violence are more	(F)	likely to drop out of high school before graduation than their peers.

A. Only A-E
B. Only A-E and B-D
C. Only B-D and C-F
D. A-E, B-D and C-F
E. None of these

Answer: D

Explanation:

Checking A-E:

The audience gave the veteran musician a standing ovation.

The above sentence is correct both grammatically and contextually. Hence, the pair A-E is valid.

Checking B-D:

Kudumbashree is one of the largest women- empowerment projects in the country today and covers over 50 per cent of Kerala households.

The above sentence is correct both grammatically and contextually. Hence, the pair B-D is valid.

Checking C-F:

Children who have been victims of violence are more likely to drop out of high school before graduation than their peers.

The above sentence is correct both grammatically and contextually. Hence, the pair C-F is valid.

Hence, option D is the correct answer.

Question 3:

Column (1)		**Column (2)**	
(A)	The tsunami swept over the island	(D)	will spur more Indian entrepreneurship.
(B)	The printer was out of ink and	(E)	hence showed promise of growth and vitality.
(C)	Hopefully the momentum at both PhonePe and Paytm	(F)	and destroyed over 2 billion dollars of property.

A. Only A-F
B. Only A-F and B-E
C. Only A-F and C-D
D. Only C-D
E. None of these

Answer: C

Explanation:

Checking A-F:

The tsunami swept over the island and destroyed over 2 billion dollars of property.

The above sentence is correct both grammatically and contextually. Hence, the pair A-F is valid.

Checking B-E:

The printer was out of ink and hence showed promise of growth and vitality.

Contextually speaking, the above sentence does not make any sense. Hence, the pair B-E is invalid.

Checking C-D:

Hopefully the momentum at both PhonePe and Paytm will spur more Indian entrepreneurship.

The above sentence is correct both grammatically and contextually. Hence, the pair C-D is valid.

Hence option C is the correct answer.

Question 4:

Column (1)		Column (2)	
(A)	The angry mob	(D)	on the lines of defense public sector undertakings.
(B)	The Centre is considering converting the factories into multiple companies	(E)	beat upon the thief mercilessly.
(C)	The four indicators for the hunger index	(F)	are undernourishment, child stunting, child wasting and child mortality.

A. Only A-E
B. Only B-D
C. Only C-F

D. Only B-D and C-F
E. None of these

Answer: D

Explanation:

Checking A-E:

The angry mob beat upon the thief mercilessly.

The sentence is grammatically erroneous. The correct preposition after 'beat' should have been 'up' instead of 'upon'. The pair A-E is hence invalid.

Checking B-D:

The Centre is considering converting the factories into multiple companies on the lines of defense public sector undertakings.

The above sentence is correct both grammatically and contextually. Hence, the pair B-D is valid.

Checking C-F:

The four indicators for the hunger index are undernourishment, child stunting, child wasting and child mortality.

The above sentence is correct both grammatically and contextually. Hence, the pair C-F is valid.

Hence, option D is the correct answer.

Question 5:

Column (1)		Column (2)	
(A)	My sister fought with two boys	(D)	his son failed to secure good marks of Mathematics.
(B)	The anguished cricketer lashed out	(E)	and won the surprise tests.
(C)	The father was deeply pained as	(F)	at the journalists when they went to ask him questions.

A. Only A-E
B. Only B-F
C. Only C-D
D. Only A-E and C-D
E. None of these

Answer: B

Explanation:

Checking A-E:

My sister fought with two boys and won the surprise tests.

The sentence does not make any sense contextually. The pair A-E is hence invalid.

Checking B-F:

The anguished cricketer lashed out at the journalists when they went to ask him questions.

The above sentence is correct both grammatically and contextually. Hence, the pair B-F is valid.

Checking C-D:

The father was deeply pained as his son failed to secure good marks of Mathematics.

The sentence does not make any sense grammatically. The correct preposition in front of "Mathematics" should have been 'in' instead of 'of'. The pair C-D is hence invalid.

Hence, option B is the correct answer.

Directions: Rearrange the following five sentences A, B, C, D and E in the proper sequence to form a meaningful paragraph and then answer the question given beside.

A. The Indian Meteorological Department just issued a warning saying that the storm has turned 'very severe'.

B. Fani, a cyclonic storm brewing in the Bay of Bengal, is set to hit India's eastern coast in the state of Odisha.

C. Fani can even worsen into an "extremely severe cyclone" by tomorrow.

D. Ministry of Home Affairs has ordered to release financial assistance, in advance to four states that stand threatened by the natural disaster.

E. This will prompt the government to put the National Disaster Response Force and the Indian Coast Guard on high alert.

1. Which of the following is SECOND sentence after re-arrangement?

A. C B. D C. A D. B E. E

2. Which of the following sentence is FOURTH after rearrangement?

A. E B. B C. D D. C E. A

3. Which of the following sentence is FIRST after rearrangement?

A. A B. B C. C D. D E. E

4. Which of the following is the LAST sentence after rearrangement?

A. A B. B C. C D. D E. E

5. Which of the following is THIRD sentence after rearrangement?

A. A B. B C. C D. D E. E

Correct Answers:

1	2	3	4	5
C	A	B	D	C

Common Explanations :

Connectors:

Sentence B is the appropriate opening statement which gives the introduction of Fani cyclone, which is about to hit Odisha.
Then next sentence would be sentence A, which takes it further and talks about the alarm issued by Meteorological department about the cyclone which is about to hit Odisha.

B to A:

B. Fani, a cyclonic storm brewing in the Bay of Bengal, is set to hit India's eastern coast in the state of Odisha.
A. The Indian Meteorological Department just issued a warning saying that the storm has turned 'very severe'.

A to C:

A. The Indian Meteorological Department just issued a warning saying that the storm has turned 'very severe'.
C. Fani can even worsen into an "extremely severe cyclone" by tomorrow.

C to E:

C. Fani can even worsen into an "extremely severe cyclone" by tomorrow.
E. This will prompt the government to put the National Disaster Response Force and the Indian Coast Guard on high alert.

Sentence D will be the concluding sentence.

Thus the correct sequence is BACED.

Answers :

1. The second sentence after re-arrangement is A.

   Hence option C is correct.

2. The fourth sentence after re-arrangement is E.

   Hence option A is correct.

3. The first sentence after re-arrangement is B.

   Hence option B is correct.

4. The last sentence after re-arrangement is D.

   Hence option D is correct.

5. The third sentence after re-arrangement is C.

   Hence option C is correct.

Direction: Five statements are given below, which are jumbled in any random order. These statements will form a coherent and meaningful paragraph, when arranged in the correct sequence. Arrange the sentences in the right order and answer the questions that follow.

The World Health Organization has declared India as polio-free since no new polio case has been reported in the country in the last couple of years.

A. It also gives an idea regarding the effective implementation of the government schemes in the country so that they give the desired result

B. Without participation from the general public, it would not have been possible to achieve this tremendous feat with the government schemes only.

C. India can take heart from this success and can replicate the same model for eradication of other diseases also from the country.

D. The thrust should be on educating the mass regarding the harmful effects of insects and the reasons for the growth of such insects.

E. This underlines the efforts by the Ministry of Health and Family Welfare along with the staff members at the ground level.

1. Which among the following will be the fourth sentence of the paragraph after the rearrangement?

A. H B. D C. B D. A E. None of the above

2. Which among the following will be the second sentence of the paragraph after the rearrangement?

A. D B. C C. B D. A E. E

3. Which among the following will be the fifth sentence of the paragraph after the rearrangement?

A. D B. B C. E D. C E. A

4. Which among the following will be the FIRST sentence of the paragraph after the rearrangement?

A. A B. C C. D D. E E. B

5. Which among the following will be the third sentence of the paragraph after the rearrangement?

A. A B. B C. D D. E E. C

Correct answers:

1	2	3	4	5
C	B	E	D	C

Common Explanation:

Since the first sentence is given of the paragraph, it is very easy to understand the topic of the passage which is regarding the achievement of India in eradicating polio from the country. This is the premise on which the sentences are based and they have to be rearranged accordingly.

After the given sentence, the next sentence should be based on the reason behind the success of the polio eradication scheme of the government in the country when most of the other schemes do not generally become successful in the country. Among the given options, Statement E explains the reason of such a feat as the contribution of the government as well as the ground level workers of the organization.

Connectors:

First sentence and E:

1. The World Health Organization **has declared India as polio-free** since no new polio case has been reported in the country in the last couple of years.

E. **This** underlines the efforts by the Ministry of Health and Family Welfare along with the staff members at the ground level.

E should be followed by a statement in which there is some inference for the government from the success of the polio eradication program of the government. C should come after that since it explains in detail that the government should think of replicating the same model in case of other diseases also.

Connectors:

E and C:

E: **This underlines the efforts by the Ministry of Health and Family Welfare along with the staff members at the ground level.**

C: India can take heart from **this success** and can replicate the same model for eradication of other diseases also from the country.

Now, C has explained the lesson that should be learnt from this step of the government. This must be followed by something that denotes the main issue behind such problems and the mantra for success behind such programs of the government. D explains that and comes after C.

Connectors:

C: India can take heart from this success and **can replicate the same model** for eradication of other diseases also from the country.

D: **The thrust should be on educating the mass** regarding the harmful effects of insects and the reasons for the growth of such insects.

D should be followed by a statement that denotes the importance of the step explained in this sentence i.e. the participation of general public in the eradication drive of any program. B explains the importance of participation of people and should follow D.

Connectors:

D: **The thrust should be on educating the mass** regarding the harmful effects of insects and the reasons for the growth of such insects.

B: **Without participation from the general public, it would not have been possible** to achieve this tremendous feat with the government schemes only.

A will come at the end of the passage as it underlines the lesson that should be internalized by the government from the model in which polio eradication drive has been launched in the country.

This makes the correct sequence of statements as: **ECDBA**

Explanations:

1.

The correct sequence of sentences is **ECDBA.**

So, B is the fourth sentence of the paragraph after the rearrangement.

It makes option C the correct choice among the given options.

2.

The correct sequence of sentences is **ECDBA.**

So, C is the second sentence of the paragraph after the rearrangement.

It makes option B the correct choice among the given options.

3.

The correct sequence of sentences is **ECDBA.**

So, A is the fifth sentence of the paragraph after the rearrangement.

It makes option E the correct choice among the given options.

4.

The correct sequence of sentences is **ECDBA**.

So, E is the first sentence of the paragraph after the rearrangement.

It makes option D the correct choice among the given options.

5.

The correct sequence of sentences is **ECDBA**.

So, D is the third sentence of the paragraph after the rearrangement.

It makes option C the correct choice among the given options.

Direction(1-10): In each of the following questions, two statements and five connectors are given. Only one of the connectors from those given can be used to combine the given two statements into one sentence without changing the meaning. Choose that connector as your answer.

1. I. The school has the best research infrastructure in the town.
II. The students are not at all interested in pursuing education.
A. Owing to B. Hence C. Because of
D. However E. None of the above

2. I. I didn't want to get into the depth of the matter at any cost.
II. I took the book from the shelf and started reading with great attention.
A. Instead B. In contrast C. On the other hand
D. However E. None of the above

3. I. I am of the opinion that there is no problem with his technique to play the short ball.
II. I will talk to him about this the first thing after the match today.
A. Nonetheless B. Because C. Hence
D. By comparison E. None of the above

4. I. The monsoon has been very late this year and it has only started raining now.
II. The farmers are demanding compensation from the government for their revenue loss.
A. Nevertheless B. Though C. Owing to
D. Yet E. None of the above

5. I. The team played its heart out in the match.
II. The result had nothing to show for the efforts put into the match by them.
A. Nonetheless B. Since C. As
D. Because E. None of the above

6. I. The office has got the best staff in the town for this job.
II. The higher management is not at all interested in its development.
A. By virtue of B. By comparison C. On the contrary
D. However E. None of the above

7. I. Utility employees should not be made to resign from the company at any cost.
II. In the long run the company is bound to suffer.
A. Nevertheless B. Otherwise C. In any case
D. Instead E. None of the above

8. I. The notification by the Reserve Bank of India to do away with stapling of currency notes by banks has not done much difference.

II. Banks are left with no other option but to issue the old notes to their customers in the absence of fresh notes from the RBI
A. Due to B. Because of C. As
D. Hence E. None of the above

9. I. I am of the opinion that my father would have done it the same way had he known this fact.
II. The differences we had when he was alive.

A. Due to
B. Instead of
C. Because of
D. As
E. Since

10. I. The popularity of cricket eating into the share of revenue of other sports in India for many years now.

II. All other sports are suffering and India is not able to win medals in Olympics in all such sports.

A. Because of
B. Therefore
C. Henceforth
D. Due to
E. None of the above

Directions (11-40): You are required to match statements from columns 1 and 2 and find which of the following pairs of statement make sense meaningfully and grammatically.

11.

Column (1)			Column (2)	
(A)	JPMorgan has been testing other technologies to		(D)	that the movie is awful.
(B)	Having had the pleasure of getting acquainted		(E)	lure consumers to spend more on its cards.
(C)	My unbiased opinion is		(F)	with him, I can vouch for his frank.

A. Only A-E
B. Only B-F
C. Only B-F, C-D
D. Only A-E, C-D
E. None of these

12.

Column (1)			Column (2)	
(A)	India is reviewing an audit report on data practices of WhatsApp Inc. to ensure compliance		(D)	but he fainted out of shock.
(B)	The bullet had barely grazed his forehead		(E)	be used to make chemical productivity.
(C)	It is only recently that crude oil has come to		(F)	with local rules before permitting a nationwide debut of the company's long-delayed payments service.

A. Only A-F
B. Only B-D
C. Only B-D, C-E
D. Only A-F, B-D
E. None of these

13.

Column (1)			Column (2)	
(A)	It appears that photo-messaging app Instagram desires		(D)	her to decline his invitation.
(B)	It is very impolite of		(E)	hotel I have ever stayed at.
(C)	This by far is one of the nicest		(F)	to work closely with new-age publishers, like meme-creators.

A. Only B-D
B. Only C-E
C. Only A-F, C-E
D. Only A-F, B-D
E. None of these

14.

Column (1)			Column (2)	
(A)	Handset makers are racing to launch their first smartphones with folding screens but analysts		(D)	to go to the concert.
(B)	I had half a mind		(E)	tangled in the most unfortunate manner.
(C)	The fates of the two brothers were		(F)	warn that the technology is still too rudimentary and expensive to woo consumers in large numbers for now.

A. Only C-E
B. A-F, B-D, C-E
C. Only B-D
D. Only A-F, C-E
E. None of these

15.

Column (1)			Column (2)	
(A)	Integrated training will motivate and equip teachers		(D)	that I knew the answer.
(B)	If you ever happen to meet Mrs. Rosely,		(E)	to encourage and foster critical thinking in students.
(C)	He took it for granted		(F)	please let her know that I am miss her terribly.

A. Only A-E
B. Only B-F
C. Only A-E, C-D
D. Only A-E, B-F, C-D
E. None of these

16.

Column (1)			Column (2)	
(A)	Soft tissue massage to the damaged area breaks down scar tissue and stimulates the production		(D)	unfamiliar man with a knife and robbed of his money.
(B)	Tom was threatened by an		(E)	than it started raining.
(C)	Hardly had we stepped out of the building		(F)	of more collagen through a combination of cell stimulation and collagen fibre cycling.

A. Only A-F
B. Only B-D
C. Only B-D, C-E
D. Only A-F, B-D
E. None of these

17.

Column (1)			Column (2)	
(A)	There is a risk that the related party may be given undue		(D)	had a happy future behind of him.
(B)	The movie tugged at all the right chords to		(E)	favours, harming the interests of the company and its shareholders.
(C)	The mother hoped that her son		(F)	make the audience cry their hearts out.

A. Only A-E
B. Only B-F
C. Only A-E, B-F
D. Only B-F, C-D
E. None of these

18.

Column (1)			Column (2)	
(A)	In the long run, the coming together of the two Asian giants		(D)	map designate rivers.
(B)	It was a worthwhile effort		(E)	is likely to bode well for other Asian oil importers too.
(C)	The blue lines on the		(F)	that rest is necessary for the well-being.

A. Only B-F
B. Only A-E
C. Only A-E, C-D
D. Only C-D
E. None of these

19.

Column (1)			Column (2)	
(A)	The person behind the fake account disguised himself		(D)	she managed to study and score good marks.
(B)	It is impossible to sleep with		(E)	as hospital staff and did not disclose that he was a consultant.
(C)	In spite of the ruckus going on in her family		(F)	all this commotion going on.

A. Only C-D
B. A-E, B-F, C-D
C. Only B-F
D. Only A-E, C-D
E. None of these

20.

Column (1)			Column (2)	
(A)	When we choose a stent for a patient, it depends on the		(D)	but the heart of a devil.
(B)	She had the looks of an angel		(E)	chirping of the birds at the crack in dawn.
(C)	We were woken up by the		(F)	science, research, and technology invested in manufacturing it.

A. Only A-F
B. Only B-D
C. Only B-D, C-E
D. Only A-F, B-D
E. None of these

21.

Column (1)			Column (2)	
(A)	The automobile industry employs 37 million		(D)	and it was a lovely sight.
(B)	Suddenly the lights went out		(E)	people and contributes to seven percent of the country's GDP.
(C)	The waves were crashing on the shore		(F)	dust finally settled.

A. Only A-E
B. Only B-F
C. Only C-D, B-F
D. Only A-E, C-D
E. None of these

22.

Column (1)			Column (2)	
(A)	The International Monetary Fund has already		(D)	dancer than a singer.
(B)	She has started to gain weight suddenly		(E)	pared India's growth projections citing lowered domestic demand.
(C)	I would rather be a		(F)	the wild elephant was no longer sane.

A. Only A-E
B. Only B-F
C. Only B-F, C-D
D. Only A-E, C-D
E. None of these

23.

Column (1)			Column (2)	
(A)	Entering into parallel pecuniary relationships with stakeholders can be detrimental		(D)	was summoned for a hearing.
(B)	We thought he loved her but it		(E)	to the interests of a company, given that such parties influence decision making.
(C)	She always speaks to him		(F)	turned out that he loved another girl.

A. Only C-D
B. Only A-E
C. Only A-E, B-F
D. Only B-F
E. None of these

24.

Column (1)			Column (2)	
(A)	The US had given a conditional waiver		(D)	than I had initially thought it would be.
(B)	The scores are low because the		(E)	task is cognitively demanding.
(C)	Writing a list of random sentences is harder		(F)	to eight nations to keep buying oil from Iran.

A. Only C-D
B. A-F, B-E, C-D
C. Only B-E
D. Only A-F, C-D
E. None of these

25.

Column (1)			Column (2)	
(A)	Trade secrets could be anything ranging from		(D)	she wanted to buy a jumpsuit.
(B)	Despite knowing that it won't suit her		(E)	and he went to the theatre instead.
(C)	He was supposed to go to school		(F)	designs and processes to methods or information.

A. Only A-F
B. Only B-D
C. Only A-F, C-E
D. Only A-F, B-D
E. None of these

26.

Column (1)			Column (2)	
(A)	When the pace of flow of wealth upwards exceeds the pace of		(D)	the dentist however he went anyway.
(B)	Though he didn't want to go to		(E)	respected by everybody.
(C)	He is a scientist who is		(F)	flow downwards, it accumulates in one part, preventing healthy circulation.

A. Only A-F
B. Only B-D
C. Only C-E, B-D
D. Only A-F, C-E
E. None of these

27.

Column (1)			Column (2)	
(A)	The need of the hour is to use the best available external clinical		(D)	car door slammed shut on his hand.
(B)	If she thinks this forum is just		(E)	evidence from systematic research before such decisions are made.
(C)	When he was little he had a		(F)	they were all carried away.

A. Only A-E
B. Only B-F
C. Only B-F, C-D
D. Only A-E, C-D
E. None of these

28.

	Column (1)			Column (2)
(A)	The usual thumb rule is that the policy response to a structural slowdown is		(D)	mood if you let it get to you.
(B)	We saw a fish splashing in the water		(E)	playing with the sand castle.
(C)	A song can make or break your		(F)	through economic reforms that ease supply constraints.

A. Only B-E
B. Only A-F
C. Only A-F, C-D
D. Only C-D
E. None of these

29.

	Column (1)			Column (2)
(A)	CART online service has a captioner that remotely listens and transcribes		(D)	everyone laughed out of courtesy.
(B)	No matter how lame the jokes were		(E)	many people saw him there.
(C)	In spite of him saying he was not there yesterday		(F)	all the spoken words in the room, and the transcription shows up on his laptop screen.

A. Only C-E
B. A-F, B-D, C-E
C. Only B-D
D. Only A-F, C-E
E. None of these

30.

	Column (1)			Column (2)
(A)	Google has decided to do away with the naming of		(D)	June since the thirties.
(B)	We were dressed to go out for dinner		(E)	its operating system based on dessert names .
(C)	This is the driest month of		(F)	standing at the edge of the world.

A. Only A-E
B. Only B-F
C. Only A-E, C-D
D. Only A-E, B-F, C-D
E. None of these

31.

	Column (1)			Column (2)
(A)	Indian stock markets are expected to continue to rise following liquidity		(D)	to share is no longer coherence.
(B)	The Red Cross constantly supplies		(E)	food to the disaster areas.
(C)	The memory we used		(F)	support by Reserve Bank of India and firm global cues.

A. Only A-F
B. Only C-D
C. Only A-F, B-E
D. Only A-F, B-E, C-D
E. None of these

32.

	Column (1)			Column (2)
(A)	Crude oil prices recovered some ground		(D)	we realise we are all the same.
(B)	His blue coat was dirty		(E)	after significant losses the previous day.
(C)	Let's all be unique together until		(F)	neatly folded and kept.

A. Only A-E
B. Only B-F
C. Only A-E, C-D
D. Only B-F, C-D
E. None of these

33.

	Column (1)			Column (2)
(A)	Global markets had been roiled at the start of the		(D)	glass else you'll hurt yourself.
(B)	He wasn't looking forward		(E)	week by new tariffs from the world's two largest economies.
(C)	Don't step on the broken		(F)	to this meeting but putting on his best behaviour anyway.

A. Only B-F
B. Only A-E
C. Only A-E, C-D
D. Only C-D
E. None of these

34.

Column (1)			Column (2)	
(A)	RBI in its third Bi-monthly Monetary Policy review has reduced its		(D)	so as to get really good seats.
(B)	Paraphrasing is all well and good as long		(E)	as you don't have the original sentence in sight when you seek to paraphrase.
(C)	They arrived early		(F)	key policy rate by an unorthodox 35 basis points.

A. Only C-D
B. A-F, B-E, C-D
C. Only B-E
D. Only A-F, C-D
E. None of these

35.

Column (1)			Column (2)	
(A)	Tom couldn't care		(D)	is focusing on reskilling teaching workforce.
(B)	In a bid to boost education and employment, HRD Ministry		(E)	they would take your teeth and leave chocolate for you.
(C)	If the Easter Bunny and the Tooth Fairy had babies		(F)	less than the previous one.

A. Only A-F
B. Only B-D
C. Only B-D, C-E
D. Only A-F, B-D, C-E
E. None of these

36.

Column (1)			Column (2)	
(A)	He thought of becoming a painter		(D)	permit the fibres to elongate and then return to the normal length.
(B)	The collagen fibres are cross-linked with chemical bridges which		(E)	he would have not passed the class.
(C)	He turned in the research paper on Friday otherwise		(F)	then the dog died.

A. Only A-F
B. Only B-D
C. Only A-F, C-E
D. Only B-D, C-E
E. None of these

37.

Column (1)			Column (2)	
(A)	Her mother is a beautiful woman		(D)	housing finance institutions both at local as well as regional levels.
(B)	NHB is an apex agency that operates as a principal agency to promote		(E)	one can find everything one needs under one roof.
(C)	Malls are great places to shop as		(F)	spewing water everywhere.

A. Only A-F
B. Only B-D
C. Only B-D, C-E
D. Only A-F, B-D
E. None of these

38.

Column (1)			Column (2)	
(A)	Strategic minerals play substantial role to play in development and security		(D)	because Delia's allergic to them.
(B)	Sometimes it is better to just walk away from things		(E)	of the nation and play critical role in the development of the national economy.
(C)	I've left out the nuts in this recipe		(F)	and go back to them later when you're in a better frame in mind.

A. Only B-F
B. Only A-E
C. Only A-E, C-D
D. Only B-F
E. None of these

39.

Column (1)			Column (2)	
(A)	I've put money aside in case I run into		(D)	management, seller support, and warehousing support.
(B)	The support provided includes product cataloguing, account		(E)	it's better to stay away from it.
(C)	If you don't like something,		(F)	some unforeseen problem in the future.

A. Only C-E
B. A-F, B-D, C-E
C. Only B-D
D. Only A-F, C-E
E. None of these

40.

	Column (1)			Column (2)
(A)	While the causes of back pain may not always be known, it is almost always accompanied		(D)	Jill running out of the room.
(B)	We sang Christmas songs in the		(E)	car all the way to Jim's house.
(C)	Jack made the sugar cookies		(F)	by weak and tight abdominal and para-spinal muscles.

A. Only A-F
B. Only B-E
C. Only A-F, C-D
D. Only A-F, B-E
E. None of these

41.

	Column (1)			Column (2)
(A)	The NCLAT had held that Essar Steel's operational creditors be treated on par		(D)	So many measures were taken.
(B)	she needs to quit worrying		(E)	then and now is inflation.
(C)	The biggest differentiator between		(F)	with financial creditors when settling the claims.

A. Only A-F
B. Only B-D
C. Only B-D, C-E
D. Only A-F, C-E
E. None of these

42.

	Column (1)			Column (2)
(A)	Infosys Foundation's FCRA licence now stands		(D)	only coming out to breathe in air.
(B)	He ran out of money,		(E)	cancelled after the Ministry agreed to accept its request.
(C)	We went to a Japanese restaurant		(F)	so he had to stop playing poker.

A. Only A-E
B. Only B-F
C. Only B-F, C-D
D. Only A-E, B-F
E. None of these

43.

Column (1)			Column (2)	
(A)	The old power structure of world oil		(D)	in the clear night sky.
(B)	The stars are twinkling		(E)	the garbage needed picking up.
(C)	Harry wanted Sally to take out		(F)	markets could be on the verge of a potentially far-reaching shift.

A. Only B-D
B. Only A-F
C. Only A-F, C-E
D. Only C-E
E. None of these

44.

Column (1)			Column (2)	
(A)	India has been striving to reduce supply risks in the		(D)	she went to the movie alone.
(B)	Since everyone was busy		(E)	the main point of what he said.
(C)	I couldn't even understand		(F)	backdrop of rising geopolitical uncertainties.

A. Only C-E
B. A-F, B-D, C-E
C. Only B-D
D. Only A-F, C-E
E. None of these

45.

Column (1)			Column (2)	
(A)	The case filed by it had accused TCS		(D)	that he was still alive.
(B)	We checked to make sure		(E)	lose around my waist.
(C)	This is a little bit too		(F)	of stealing its intellectual property.

A. Only A-F
B. Only B-D
C. Only A-F, C-E
D. Only A-F, B-D
E. None of these

46.

	Column (1)			Column (2)
(A)	Concepts like fairness, justice and		(D)	stuffed them into the suitcase.
(B)	She folded her clothes and		(E)	left of the cupboard is the sink.
(C)	That old lasso is on the		(F)	morality are beyond the domain of economic analysis.

A. Only A-F
B. Only B-D
C. Only A-F, B-D
D. Only A-F, B-D, C-E
E. None of these

47.

	Column (1)			Column (2)
(A)	Perfectionists often find themselves unable to cope		(D)	themselves ran away.
(B)	They asked us to go to Boston with		(E)	to make ends meet.
(C)	She works two jobs		(F)	with even small frustrations, failures and losses.

A. Only A-F
B. Only B-D
C. Only B-D, C-E
D. Only A-F, C-E
E. None of these

48.

	Column (1)			Column (2)
(A)	A whole sports stadium was required to assemble the		(D)	certainly goes a long way.
(B)	Creativity and uniqueness		(E)	seemed like an excuse.
(C)	Her reason for not having time to join us		(F)	thousands of small investors in the Reliance enterprise.

A. Only B-D
B. Only A-F
C. Only A-F, C-E, B-D
D. Only C-E, A-F
E. None of these

49.

Column (1)			Column (2)	
(A)	Wealth must circulate within the economy		(D)	door after the horse has been stolen.
(B)	My sister tries to be copy me by		(E)	for it to grow inclusively and sustainably.
(C)	It's too late to shut the barn		(F)	saying that she likes all the same things that I do.

A. Only C-D
B. A-E, B-F, C-D
C. Only B-F
D. Only A-E, C-D
E. None of these

50.

Column (1)			Column (2)	
(A)	Blatantly claiming that a stent is better than its foreign		(D)	and paints only with bold colours.
(B)	Romi and Mia started talking as soon		(E)	counterpart will only hurt the healthcare system in India.
(C)	She does not like pastels		(F)	the teacher entered the room.

A. Only A-E
B. Only B-F
C. Only A-E, C-D
D. Only A-E, B-F, C-D
E. None of these

Correct answers:

1	2	3	4	5	6	7	8	9	10	11	12	13	14	15	16	17	18	19	20	21	22	23	24	25
D	A	A	C	A	D	B	C	B	D	D	D	D	B	C	D	C	C	B	D	D	D	C	B	D
26	27	28	29	30	31	32	33	34	35	36	37	38	39	40	41	42	43	44	45	46	47	48	49	50
D	D	C	B	C	C	C	C	B	C	D	C	C	B	D	D	D	C	B	D	C	D	D	B	C

Explanation:

1. Here the two statements have been used in the sense that the school has the best infrastructure for conducting research but the students are not at all interested in taking advantage of that. Only however can be used to connect these two sentences since the first one is about some facility whereas the next is about how that is going in vain. All the other connectors are used to connect sentences that have cause and effect relationship between them. So, all of them can be eliminated.
The connected sentence would be: The school has the best research infrastructure in the town, **however,** the students are not at all interested in pursuing education.
This makes Option D the correct choice among the given options.

2. If we take into account the context of the two given statements, it is regarding the fact that I did not want to listen to the matter and started reading the book. In contrast is not correct because it is used to indicate something that is opposite to the other and it is certainly not fit in the given context. On the other hand and however can also be eliminated since they cannot connect these two given statements. Only instead can be used in order to connect the two sentences without changing the meaning.
The connected statement would be: I didn't want to get into the depth of the matter at any cost, **instead,** I took the book from the shelf and started reading with great attention.
This makes Option A the correct choice among the given options.

3. The two statements are regarding the context that the person does not think that there is no problem with his technique to play the short ball but he will definitely talk about it with him after the match. Among the given connectors, both because and hence are mainly used for statements that have cause and effect relationship whereas by comparison is used in order to indicate any kind of comparison. Only nonetheless can connect these two statements since it implies in spite of that and that is why it can be used to connect these two statements without changing the meaning.
The connected sentence would be: I am of the opinion that there is no problem with his technique to play the short ball, **nonetheless,** I will talk to him about this the first thing after the match today.
This makes Option A the correct choice among the given options.

4. Here the given two statements carry a cause and effect relationship. The reason the farmers are asking for compensation is because of the late onset of monsoon in the country. That is the main reason the farmers have lost their revenue. Among the given connectors, we can see that nevertheless can be used to indicate that in spite of something we have done something else whereas though and yet are also not correct here. There is only one connector that can be used here i.e. owing to.

The connected sentence would be: **Owing to** the late monsoon and rains this year, the farmers are demanding compensation from the government for their revenue loss.

This makes Option C the correct choice among the given options.

5. According to the given context we can see that the players in the team played very well but at the end of the day they lost of the match. Therefore nothing could be shown against the efforts put forward by the players in the match. Nonetheless is used to imply in spite of whereas the rest of the three connectors are mainly used for the purpose of connecting the cause and effect related sentences.

The connected sentence would be:

The team played its heart out in the match, **nonetheless,** the result had nothing to show for the efforts put into the match by them.

This makes Option A the correct choice among the given options.

6. It can be understood that the two sentences can be connected in order to imply that the office can do well but the management is not that interested to pursue the same. That is why in spite of having good and dedicated staff under its belt, it has failed to produce wonderful results. Among the given connecting words, we can use however in order to connect the sentences without changing the meaning. By virtue of means because of something, by comparison implies comparing something whereas on the contrary refers to being the opposite of something.

The connected sentence would be:

The office has got the best staff in the town for this job, **however**, the higher management is not at all interested in its development.

This makes Option D the correct choice among the given options.

7. Here we are talking about the fact that if the employees are not made to stay back it is bound that the organization will suffer in the long run. Therefore the relation is regarding the cause and effect here. Nevertheless implies in spite of something whereas instead is used to connect sentences that have the relation regarding in place of something.

The connected sentence would be:

Utility employees should not be made to resign from the company at any cost, **otherwise,** in the long run the company is bound to suffer.

This makes Option B the correct choice among the given options.

8. If we read the two sentences they are connected by the cause and effect relationship where one is the reason and the other is the result of something. Among the given options, 'as' is the correct choice since it connects the sentences as cause and effect.

Combining the two sentences the new sentence will be:

As banks are left with no other option but to issue the old notes to their customers in the absence of fresh notes from the RBI, the notification by the Reserve Bank of India to do away with stapling off currency notes by banks has not done much difference.

So, Option C is the right choice among the given options.

9. If we read the sentences it is clear that it talks about two contrasting things. Among the given choices, 'instead of' is the right fit as it means that 'despite the fact that'.

Combing the two sentences the new statement will be:

Instead of the differences we had when he was alive, I am of the opinion that my father would have done it the same way had he known this fact.

So, Option B is the right choice.

10. If we read the two sentences, we shall observe that they are connected by the cause and effect relationship. Hence, 'due to' will be the perfect fit in the given context as it means that 'for this reason'.

Combing the two sentences the new sentence will be:

Due to the popularity of cricket eating into the share of revenue of other sports in India for many years now, all other sports are suffering and India is not able to win medals in Olympics in all such sports.

So, Option D is the correct choice among the given options.

11. **Checking A-E:**

JPMorgan has been testing other technologies to lure consumers to spend more on its cards.

The above sentence is correct both grammatically and contextually.

Checking B-F:

Having had the pleasure of getting acquainted with him, I can vouch for his frank.

The above sentence is incorrect grammatically because 'frankness' should have been used instead of 'frank'.

Checking C-D:

My unbiased opinion is that the movie is awful.

The above sentence too is correct both grammatically and contextually.

Option D is hence the correct answer.

12. **Checking A-F:**

India is reviewing an audit report on data practices of WhatsApp Inc. to ensure compliance with local rules before permitting a nationwide debut of the company's long-delayed payments service.

The above sentence is correct both grammatically and contextually.

Checking B-D:

The bullet had barely grazed his forehead but he fainted out of shock.

The above sentence is also correct both grammatically and contextually.

Checking C-E:

It is only recently that crude oil has come to be used to make chemical productivity.

The above sentence is incorrect grammatically. 'Products' should have been used instead of 'productivity' in order to make the sentence correct.

Option D is hence the correct answer.

13. **Checking B-D:**

It is very impolite of her to decline his invitation.

The above sentence is correct both grammatically and contextually.

Checking C-E:

This by far is one of the nicest hotel I have ever stayed at.

The above sentence is incorrect grammatically as the phrase 'one of' is always followed by a plural noun which is not the case here.

Checking A-F:

It appears that photo-messaging app Instagram desires to work closely with new-age publishers, like meme-creators.

The above sentence is correct both grammatically and contextually.

Option D is hence the correct answer.

14. **Checking A-F:**

Handset makers are racing to launch their first smartphones with folding screens but analysts warn that the technology is still too rudimentary and expensive to woo consumers in large numbers for now.

The above sentence is correct both grammatically and contextually.

Checking B-D:

I had half a mind to go to the concert.

The above sentence is correct both grammatically and contextually as well.

Checking C-E:

The fates of the two brothers were tangled in the most unfortunate manner.

The above sentence too is correct both grammatically and contextually.

Option B is hence the correct answer.

15. **Checking A-E:**

Integrated training will motivate and equip teachers to encourage and foster critical thinking in students.

The above sentence is correct both grammatically and contextually.

Checking B-F:

If you ever happen to meet Mrs. Rosely, please let her know that I am miss her terribly.

The above sentence is grammatically incorrect because 'missing' should be used after be verb instead of 'miss'.

Checking C-D:

He took it for granted that I knew the answer.

The above sentence is also correct both grammatically and contextually.

Option C is hence the correct answer.

16. **Checking A-F:**

Soft tissue massage to the damaged area breaks down scar tissue and stimulates the production of more collagen through a combination of cell stimulation and collagen fibre cycling.

The above sentence is correct both grammatically and contextually.

Checking B-D:

Tom was threatened by an unfamiliar man with a knife and robbed of his money.

The above sentence is also correct both grammatically and contextually.

Checking C-E:

Hardly had we stepped out of the building than it started raining.

The above sentence is incorrect grammatically because the conjunction 'hardly' is paired with 'when' and not 'than'.

Option D is hence the correct answer.

17. **Checking A-E:**

There is a risk that the related party may be given undue favours, harming the interests of the company and its shareholders.

The above sentence is correct both grammatically and contextually.

Checking B-F:

The movie tugged at all the right chords to make the audience cry their hearts out.

The above sentence too is correct both grammatically and contextually. Hence, the pair B-F is valid.

Checking C-D:

The mother hoped that her son had a happy future behind of him.

The above sentence is contextually incorrect because 'ahead' should have been used after 'future' instead of 'behind'.

Option C is hence the correct answer.

18. **Checking B-F:**

It was a worthwhile effort that rest is necessary for the well-being.

The sentence doesn't make any sense contextually. The pair B-F is hence invalid.

Checking A-E:

In the long run, the coming together of the two Asian giants is likely to bode well for other Asian oil importers too.

The above sentence is correct both grammatically and contextually.

Checking C-D:

The blue lines on the map designate rivers.

The above sentence is also correct both grammatically and contextually.

Option C is hence the correct answer.

19. **Checking A-E:**

The person behind the fake account disguised himself as hospital staff and did not disclose that he was a consultant.

The above sentence is correct both grammatically and contextually.

Checking B-F:

It is impossible to sleep with all this commotion going on.

The above sentence is correct both grammatically and contextually as well.

Checking C-D:

In spite of the ruckus going on in her family she managed to study and score good marks.

The above sentence too is correct both grammatically and contextually.

Option B is hence the correct answer.

20. **Checking A-F:**

When we choose a stent for a patient, it depends on the science, research, and technology invested in manufacturing it.

The above sentence is correct both grammatically and contextually.

Checking B-D:

She had the looks of an angel but the heart of a devil.

The above sentence is also correct both grammatically and contextually.

Checking C-E:

We were woken up by the chirping of the birds at the crack in dawn.

The above sentence is grammatically incorrect because of the usage of the preposition 'in' before dawn. Instead of 'in' 'of' should have been used.

Option D is hence the correct answer.

21. **Checking B-F:**

Suddenly the lights went out dust finally settled.

The sentence doesn't make any sense. The pair B-F is hence invalid.

Checking A-E:

The automobile industry employs 37 million people and contributes to seven percent of the country's GDP.

The above sentence is correct both grammatically and contextually.

Checking C-D:

The waves were crashing on the shore and it was a lovely sight.

The above sentence too is correct both grammatically and contextually.

Option D is hence the correct answer.

22. **Checking B-F:**

She has started to gain weight suddenly the wild elephant was no longer sane.

The sentence doesn't make any sense. The pair B-F is hence invalid.

Checking A-E:

The International Monetary Fund has already pared India's growth projections citing lowered domestic demand.

The above sentence is correct both grammatically and contextually.

Checking C-D:

I would rather be a dancer than a singer.

The above sentence too is correct both grammatically and contextually.

Option D is hence the correct answer.

23. **Checking C-D:**

She always speaks to him was summoned for a hearing.

The sentence doesn't make any sense contextually. The pair A-E is hence invalid.

Checking A-E:

Entering into parallel pecuniary relationships with stakeholders can be detrimental to the interests of a company, given that such parties influence decision making.

The above sentence is correct both grammatically and contextually.

Checking B-F:

We thought he loved her but it turned out that he loved another girl.

The above sentence is also correct both grammatically and contextually.

Option C is hence the correct answer.

24. Checking A-F:

The US had given a conditional waiver to eight nations to keep buying oil from Iran.

The above sentence is correct both grammatically and contextually.

Checking B-E:

The scores are low because the task is cognitively demanding.

The above sentence is correct both grammatically and contextually as well.

Checking C-D:

Writing a list of random sentences is harder than I had initially thought it would be.

The above sentence too is correct both grammatically and contextually.

Option B is hence the correct answer.

25. Checking A-F:

Trade secrets could be anything ranging from designs and processes to methods or information.

The above sentence is correct both grammatically and contextually.

Checking B-D:

Despite knowing that it won't suit her she wanted to buy a jumpsuit.

The above sentence is also correct both grammatically and contextually.

Checking C-E:

He was supposed to go to school and he went to the theatre instead.

Here, as the sentence implies contrast in ideas, usage of the conjunction 'and' is absurd. Instead of 'and' 'but' should have been used. Hence, the sentence doesn't make any sense. The pair C-E is hence invalid.

Option D is hence the correct answer.

26. Checking A-F:

When the pace of flow of wealth upwards exceeds the pace of flow downwards, it accumulates in one part, preventing healthy circulation.

The above sentence is correct both grammatically and contextually.

Checking B-D:

Though he didn't want to go to the dentist however he went anyway.

The above sentence is incorrect grammatically. The conjunction though should be paired with 'yet' instead of 'however'.

Checking C-E:

He is a scientist who is respected by everybody.

The above sentence too is correct both grammatically and contextually.

Option D is hence the correct answer.

27. **Checking A-E:**

The need of the hour is to use the best available external clinical evidence from systematic research before such decisions are made.

The above sentence is correct both grammatically and contextually

Checking B-F:

If she thinks this forum is just they were all carried away.

The sentence doesn't make any sense contextually. The pair B-F is hence invalid.

Checking C-D:

When he was little he had a car door slammed shut on his hand.

The above sentence too is correct both grammatically and contextually. Hence, the pair C-D is valid.

Option D is hence the correct answer.

28. **Checking B-E:**

We saw a fish splashing in the water playing with the sand castle.

The sentence doesn't make any sense contextually. The pair B-E is hence invalid.

Checking A-F:

The usual thumb rule is that the policy response to a structural slowdown is through economic reforms that ease supply constraints.

The above sentence is correct both grammatically and contextually.

Checking C-D:

A song can make or break your mood if you let it get to you.

The above sentence is also correct both grammatically and contextually.

Option C is hence the correct answer.

29. **Checking A-F:**

CART online service has a captioner that remotely listens and transcribes all the spoken words in the room, and the transcription shows up on his laptop screen.

The above sentence is correct both grammatically and contextually.

Checking B-D:

No matter how lame the jokes were everyone laughed out of courtesy.

The above sentence is correct both grammatically and contextually as well.

Checking C-E:

In spite of him saying he was not there yesterday many people saw him there.

The above sentence too is correct both grammatically and contextually.

Option B is hence the correct answer.

30. **Checking A-E:**

Google has decided to do away with the naming of its operating system based on dessert names .

The above sentence is correct both grammatically and contextually.

Checking B-F:

We were dressed to go out for dinner standing at the edge of the world.

The sentence doesn't make any sense. The pair B-F is hence invalid.

Checking C-D:

This is the driest month of June since the thirties.

The above sentence is also correct both grammatically and contextually.

Option C is hence the correct answer.

31. **Checking C-D:**

The memory we used to share is no longer coherence.

The above sentence is grammatically incorrect because the adjective 'coherent' should have been used instead of the noun 'coherence'.

Checking A-F:

Indian stock markets are expected to continue to rise following liquidity support by Reserve Bank of India and firm global cues.

The above sentence is correct both grammatically and contextually.

Checking B-E:

The Red Cross constantly supplies food to the disaster areas.

The above sentence too is correct both grammatically and contextually.

Option C is hence the correct answer.

32. **Checking A-E:**

Crude oil prices recovered some ground after significant losses the previous day.

The above sentence is correct both grammatically and contextually.

Checking B-F:

His blue coat was dirty neatly folded and kept.

The sentence doesn't make any sense contextually. The pair B-F is hence invalid.

Checking C-D:

Let's all be unique together until we realise we are all the same.

The above sentence too is correct both grammatically and contextually. Hence, the pair C-D is valid.

Option C is hence the correct answer.

33. **Checking B-F:**

He wasn't looking forward to this meeting but putting on his best behaviour anyway.

The above sentence is incorrect grammatically as 'put' should have been used instead of 'putting'.

Checking A-E:

Global markets had been roiled at the start of the week by new tariffs from the world's two largest economies.

The above sentence is correct both grammatically and contextually.

Checking C-D:

Don't step on the broken glass else you'll hurt yourself.

The above sentence is also correct both grammatically and contextually.

Option C is hence the correct answer.

34. **Checking A-F:**

RBI in its third Bi-monthly Monetary Policy review has reduced its key policy rate by an unorthodox 35 basis points.

The above sentence is correct both grammatically and contextually.

Checking B-D:

Paraphrasing is all well and good as long as you don't have the original sentence in sight when you seek to paraphrase.

The above sentence is correct both grammatically and contextually as well.

Checking C-E:

They arrived early so as to get really good seats.

The above sentence too is correct both grammatically and contextually.

Option B is hence the correct answer.

35. **Checking A-F:**

Tom couldn't care less than the previous one.

The sentence doesn't make any sense. The pair A-F is hence invalid.

Checking B-D:

In a bid to boost education and employment, HRD Ministry is focusing on reskilling teaching workforce.

The above sentence is correct both grammatically and contextually.

Checking C-E:

More and more parents are encouraging their children to play and seek a career of sports.

If the Easter Bunny and the Tooth Fairy had babies they would take your teeth and leave chocolate for you.

Option C is hence the correct answer.

36. **Checking A-F:**

He thought of becoming a painter then the dog died.

The sentence doesn't make any sense. The pair A-F is hence invalid.

Checking B-D:

The collagen fibres are cross-linked with chemical bridges which permit the fibres to elongate and then return to the normal length.

The above sentence is correct both grammatically and contextually.

Checking C-E:

He turned in the research paper on Friday otherwise he would have not passed the class.

The above sentence too is correct both grammatically and contextually.

Option D is hence the correct answer.

37. **Checking A-F:**

Her mother is a beautiful woman spewing water everywhere.

The sentence doesn't make any sense. The pair A-F is hence invalid.

Checking B-D:

NHB is an apex agency that operates as a principal agency to promote housing finance institutions both at local as well as regional levels.

The above sentence is correct both grammatically and contextually.

Checking C-E:

Malls are great places to shop as one can find everything one needs under one roof.

The above sentence too is correct both grammatically and contextually. Hence, the pair C-E is valid.

Option C is hence the correct answer.

38. **Checking B-F:**

Sometimes it is better to just walk away from things and go back to them later when you're in a better frame in mind.

The above sentence is incorrect grammatically as the correct phrase is 'frame of mind' and not 'frame in mind'.

Checking A-E:

Strategic minerals play substantial role to play in development and security of the nation and play critical role in the development of the national economy.

The above sentence is correct both grammatically and contextually.

Checking C-D:

I've left out the nuts in this recipe because Delia's allergic to them.

The above sentence is also correct both grammatically and contextually.

Option C is hence the correct answer.

39. **Checking A-F:**

I've put money aside in case I run into some unforeseen problem in the future.

The above sentence is correct both grammatically and contextually.

Checking B-D:

The support provided includes product cataloguing, account management, seller support, and warehousing support.

The above sentence is correct both grammatically and contextually as well.

Checking C-E:

If you don't like something, it's better to stay away from it.

The above sentence too is correct both grammatically and contextually.

Option B is hence the correct answer.

40. **Checking A-F:**

While the causes of back pain may not always be known, it is almost always accompanied by weak and tight abdominal and para-spinal muscles.

The above sentence is correct both grammatically and contextually.

Checking B-E:

We sang Christmas songs in the car all the way to Jim's house.

The above sentence is also correct both grammatically and contextually.

Checking C-D:

Jack made the sugar cookies Jill running out of the room.

The sentence doesn't make any sense. The pair C-D is hence invalid.

Option D is hence the correct answer.

41. **Checking B-D:**

She needs to quit worrying then and now is inflation.

The sentence doesn't make any sense. The pair B-D is hence invalid.

Checking A-F:

The NCLAT had held that Essar Steel's operational creditors be treated on par with financial creditors when settling the claims.

The above sentence is correct both grammatically and contextually.

Checking C-E:

The biggest differentiator between then and now is inflation.

The above sentence too is correct both grammatically and contextually.

Option D is hence the correct answer.

42. **Checking A-E:**

Infosys Foundation's FCRA licence now stands cancelled after the Ministry agreed to accept its request.

The above sentence is correct both grammatically and contextually.

Checking B-F:

He ran out of money, so he had to stop playing poker.

The above sentence is also correct both grammatically and contextually.

Checking C-D:

We went to a Japanese restaurant only coming out to breathe in air.

The above sentence too is incorrect both grammatically and contextually. Hence, the pair C-D is invalid.

Option D is hence the correct answer

43. **Checking A-F:**

The old power structure of world oil markets could be on the verge of a potentially far-reaching shift.

The above sentence is correct both grammatically and contextually.

Checking B-D:

The stars are twinkling in the clear night sky.

The above sentence is also correct both grammatically and contextually.

Checking C-E:

Harry wanted Sally to take out the garbage needed picking up.

The sentence doesn't make any sense contextually. The pair C-E is hence invalid.

Option c is hence the correct answer.

44. **Checking A-F:**

India has been striving to reduce supply risks in the backdrop of rising geopolitical uncertainties.

The above sentence is correct both grammatically and contextually.

Checking B-D:

Since everyone was busy she went to the movie alone.

The above sentence is correct both grammatically and

contextually as well.

Checking C-E:

I couldn't even understand the main point of what he said.

The above sentence too is correct both grammatically and contextually.

Option B is hence the correct answer.

45 Checking A-F:

The case filed by it had accused TCS of stealing its intellectual property.

The above sentence is correct both grammatically and contextually.

Checking B-D:

This is a little bit too lose around my waist.

The above sentence is incorrect. “Loose” should be used instead of “lose” in order to make it meaningfully correct.

Option D is hence the correct answer.

46. Checking A-F:

Concepts like fairness, justice and morality are beyond the domain of economic analysis.

The above sentence is correct both grammatically and contextually.

Checking B-D:

She folded her clothes and stuffed them into the suitcase.

The above sentence too is correct both grammatically and contextually.

Checking C-E:

That old lasso is on the left of the cupboard is the sink.

The sentence doesn't make any sense. The pair C-E is hence invalid.

Option C is hence the correct answer.

47. Checking A-F:

Perfectionists often find themselves unable to cope with even small frustrations, failures and losses.

The above sentence is correct both grammatically and contextually.

Checking B-D:

They asked us to go to Boston with themselves ran away.

The sentence doesn't make any sense. The pair B-D is hence invalid.

Checking C-E:

She works two jobs to make ends meet.

The above sentence too is correct both grammatically and contextually. Hence, the pair C-E is valid.

Option D is hence the correct answer.

48. **Checking B-D:**

Creativity and uniqueness certainly goes a long way.

The above sentence is incorrect grammatically as the singular verb 'goes' has been used for the plural subject 'creativity and uniqueness'.

Checking A-F:

A whole sports stadium was required to assemble the thousands of small investors in the Reliance enterprise.

The above sentence is correct both grammatically and contextually.

Checking C-E:

Her reason for not having time to join us seemed like an excuse.

The above sentence is also correct both grammatically and contextually.

Option D is hence the correct answer.

49. **Checking A-E:**

Wealth must circulate within the economy for it to grow inclusively and sustainably.

The above sentence is correct both grammatically and contextually.

Checking B-F:

My sister tries to be copy me by saying that she likes all the same things that I do.

The above sentence is correct both grammatically and contextually as well.

Checking C-D:

It's too late to shut the barn door after the horse has been stolen.

The above sentence too is correct both grammatically and contextually.

Option B is hence the correct answer.

50. **Checking A-E:**

Blatantly claiming that a stent is better than its foreign counterpart will only hurt the healthcare system in India.

The above sentence is correct both grammatically and contextually.

Checking B-F:

Romi and Mia started talking as soon the teacher entered the room.

The above sentence is grammatically incorrect because the correct conjunction is "as soon as" and not "as soon".

Checking C-D:

She does not like pastels and paints only with bold colours.

The above sentence is also correct both grammatically and contextually.

Option C is hence the correct answer.

Directions: In the following questions two columns are given containing three Sentences/phrases each. In first column, sentences/phrases are A, B and C and in the second column the sentences/phrases are D, E and F. A sentence/phrase from the first column may or may not connect with another sentence/phrase from the second column to make a grammatically and contextually correct sentence. Each question has five options, four of which display the sequence(s) in which the sentences/phrases can be joined to form a grammatically and contextually correct sentence. If none of the options given forms a correct sentence after combination, mark option (E), i.e. "None of these" as your answer.

1.

	Column (1)			Column (2)
(A)	The RBI could have addressed these concerns		(D)	to think over the sources from which it can bridge the liquidity gap.
(B)	The RBI circular had adversely impacted		(E)	when banks and borrowers from these sectors bought these issues to its notice.
(C)	This would provide time for bankers		(F)	resolution plans which were under process between lenders and debtors.

A. A-E, B-F B. C-D, B-E C. C-E D. B-F E. None of the above

2.

	Column (1)			Column (2)
(A)	The Government of India has recently passed an act		(D)	who decriminalizes suicide and empowers individuals with mental illness.
(B)	Voluntary organizations are training community workers		(E)	our ears to the emotions of our family members and neighbours.
(C)	Each of us is lending a hand, when we lend		(F)	with the requisite skills required to take care of the mentally ill.

A. A-E, B-D B. C-E, B-F C. A-D D. B-F E. None of the above

3.

	Column (1)		Column (2)
(A)	There are several multiplexes in Chhattisgarh	(D)	doesn't want to share the revenue with the producers.
(B)	The video companies are making money but they	(E)	but they don't give any priority to local films.
(C)	It took time for them to realise that	(F)	home video rights, satellite rights, digital rights are different things.

A. A-E, B-D B. C-E, B-F C. A-E, C-F D. B-F E. None of the above

4.

	Column (1)		Column (2)
(A)	Last year we performed in Fiji and	(D)	flavour which people loves.
(B)	Our music has a distinctive	(E)	used by our band is Banjo.
(C)	The most modern instrument	(F)	almost each one loved the show.

A. A-E, B-D B. C-E, B-F C. A-E, C-F D. C-E E. None of the above

5.

	Column (1)		Column (2)
(A)	Pakistan could be blacklisted	(D)	by the FATF due to lobbying by India.
(B)	The FATF is working to curb terrorism	(E)	if Pakistan is pushed into the FATF blacklist.
(C)	The Foreign office is calculating loss	(F)	financing and money laundering.

A. A-E, B-D B. C-E, B-F C. A-E, C-F D. C-E E. None of the above

6.

	Column (1)		Column (2)
(A)	Global Warming can do more than just melt polar ice and change	(D)	Shops and restaurants of airplane passengers to use.
(B)	The Earth's temperature will continue to rise	(E)	so long as mankind continues to produce greenhouse gases.
(C)	Most international airports have	(F)	weather patterns throughout the world.

A. A-F, C-D B. A-E, B-F C. A-F, B-E D. A-F, B-E, C-D E. None of these

7.

	Column (1)		Column (2)
(A)	The First World War unlike the second, can be argued as being orchestrated by not a single party or regime	(D)	new, eager men and plentiful supplies.
(B)	The goal of the United Nations is	(E)	to improve living conditions for people all over the world.
(C)	The United States entry into the war brought millions of fresh,	(F)	but through a complicated series of events which played part in tipping the fragile balance of European powers.

A. B-D B. A-F, B-E, C-D C. B-F, C-D D. A-E E. None of these

8.

	Column (1)		Column (2)
(A)	UNICEF's Supply Division is based in Copenhagen and	(D)	not flat like most birds.
(B)	A Black Hole is a great amount of	(E)	matter packed into a very small area.
(C)	Hummingbirds fly with their bodies held upright,	(F)	serves as the primary point of distribution for essential healthcare items.

A. A-F B. B-E C. C-D, B-E D. A-F, B-E, C-D E. None of these

9.

	Column (1)		Column (2)
(A)	The tortuous talks on Brexit, which are now entering a critical stage,	(D)	and marketing departments of the future cost of supplies in order to assist them in their forecasting.
(B)	Industrial purchasing may be defined as the decision-making process by	(E)	contain uncanny echoes of the events of a century ago that reshaped the continent of Europe.
(C)	Coordinate with engineering when developing specifications or advise the sales and marketing.	(F)	which formal organizations establish the need for purchased products and services.

A. C-D B. A-D, B-F C. C-F, A-D D. B-F E. None of the above

10.

	Column (1)			Column (2)
(A)	The Alaknanda is a Himalayan river in the Indian state of Uttarakhand		(D)	and one of the two headstreams of the Ganga.
(B)	Goa is India's smallest state by area and the		(E)	important religions – Buddhism and Jainism to the world.
(C)	Bihar is the remarkable state that gave two		(F)	the fourth smallest by population.

A. C-D B. C-E, A-D C. A-D, B-F D. A-E E. None of the above

Correct Answers:

1	2	3	4	5	6	7	8	9	10
D	B	C	D	E	C	B	D	D	E

Explanations:

1. A-E: The RBI could have addressed these concerns when banks and borrowers from these sectors bought these issues to its notice.

Use of verb "bought" creates an error in the sentence. "bought" is the past participle of verb "buy" is clearly a misfit here. The correct verb to be used is "brought", which is the past participle of "bring".

Correct sentence: The RBI could have addressed these concerns when banks and borrowers from these sectors **brought** these issues to its notice.

C-D: This would provide time for bankers to think over the sources from which it can bridge the liquidity gap.

This sentence seems to be contextually correct but on the grammar hand it has a problem with respect to the use of pronoun. Here "Bankers" (noun) is plural, so it will be replaced with the plural pronoun "they" instead of "it".

Correct sentence: This would provide time for bankers to think over the sources from which **they** can bridge the liquidity gap.

B- F: The RBI circular had adversely impacted resolution plans which were under process between lenders and debtors.

This make a grammatically as well as contextually correct sentence.

Hence option D is correct.

2. A-D: The Government of India has recently passed an act who decriminalizes suicide and empowers individuals with mental illness.

Here use of "who" is incorrect as it is referred to Act. 'Who' is used for living persons.

Correct sentence: The Government of India has recently passed an act **which** decriminalizes suicide and empowers individuals with mental illness.

B-F: Voluntary organizations are training community workers with the requisite skills required to take care of the mentally ill.

Some of us may confuse and match B-D, but its incorrect as community workers don't possess the authority to decriminalize or criminalize an issue.

So, the correct combination is B-F.

C-E: Each of us is lending a hand, when we lend our ears to the emotions of our family members and neighbors.
C-E is grammatically as well as contextually correct.
Hence option B is correct.

3. A-E: There are several multiplexes in Chhattisgarh but they don't give any priority to local films.

A-E forms a grammatically as well contextually correct sentence.

B-D: The video companies are making money but they doesn't want to share the revenue with the producers.

B-D make a contextually correct sentence but grammatically they don't follow the subject-verb agreement. Video companies are plural, thus helping verb should also be plural (don't instead of doesn't).

Correct Sentence: The video companies are making money but they **don't** want to share the revenue with the producers.

C-F: It took time for them to realise that home video rights, satellite rights, digital rights are different things.
C-F forms a grammatically as well contextually correct sentence.

Hence option C is correct.

4. A-F: Last year we performed in Fiji and almost each one loved the show.

Each is not used with almost as per grammar rules. Thus it should be replaced with every in order to make a grammatically correct sentence as well.

Correct sentence: Last year we performed in Fiji and almost **everyone** loved the show.

B- D: Our music has a distinctive flavour which people loves.

People is singular, thus loves needs to be "love" to make it grammatically correct.

Correct sentence: Our music has a distinctive flavour which people **love**.

C-E: The most modern instrument used by our band is Banjo.

C-E is grammatically as well as contextually correct.

Hence option D is correct.

5. A-D: Pakistan could be blacklisted by the FATF due to lobbying by India.

A-D forms a grammatically and contextually correct sentence.

B-F: The FATF is working to curb terrorism financing and money laundering.

B-F also forms a grammatically and contextually correct sentence.

C-E: The Foreign office is calculating loss if Pakistan is pushed into the FATF blacklist.

C-E also forms a grammatically and contextually correct sentence.

Hence option E is correct.

6. Let's use elimination technique to cancel the choices that are absurd or irrelevant.

A-F:

Global Warming can do more than just melt polar ice and change weather patterns throughout the world.

This is reasonably and grammatically correct sentence.

A-E:

Global Warming can do more than just melt polar ice and change so long as mankind continues to produce greenhouse gases.

The sentence after combining the fragments doesn't make sense and is hence incorrect.

B-E:

The Earth's temperature will continue to rise so long as mankind continues to produce greenhouse gases.

This complete sentence is evidently correct, both grammatically and contextually.

C-D:

Most international airports have Shops and restaurants of airplane passengers to use.

Usage of 'of 'instead of 'for' makes it erroneous and hence option A and E can be eliminated as well.

Clearly, option **C** is correct answer.

7. Let's use elimination technique to cancel the choices that are absurd or irrelevant.

A-F:
The First World War unlike the second, can be argued as being orchestrated by not a single party or regime but through a complicated series of events which played part in tipping the fragile balance of European powers.

The sentence above is evidently correct both grammatically and contextually.

B-D:
The goal of the United Nations is new, eager men and plentiful supplies.

The sentence after combining the fragments does not make sense and is hence incorrect.

B-E:
The goal of the United Nations is to improve living conditions for people all over the world.

The sentence after combining the fragments does make sense and is hence correct.

B-F:
The goal of the United Nations is but through a complicated series of events which played part in tipping the fragile balance of European powers.

The sentence after combining the fragments does not make sense and is hence incorrect. .

C-D:
The United States entry into the war brought millions of fresh, new, eager men and plentiful supplies

This sentence too is correct both grammatically and contextually.

Hence, Clearly Option **B** is correct option.

8. **A-F:**
UNICEF's Supply Division is based in Copenhagen and serves as the primary point of distribution for such essential healthcare items.

The sentence after combining the fragments does make sense and is hence correct.

B-E:
A Black Hole is a great amount of matter packed into a very small area.

The sentence after combining the fragments does make sense and is hence incorrect.

C-D:
Hummingbirds fly with their bodies held upright, not flat like most birds.

The sentence after combining the fragments does make sense and is hence correct.
Clearly, option **D** is correct answer.

9. Let's use elimination technique to cancel the choices that are absurd or irrelevant.

C-D:

Coordinate with engineering when developing specifications or advise the sales and marketing departments and marketing departments of the future cost of supplies in order to assist them in their forecasting.

The sentence above after combining the fragments doesn't make any sense. It is absurd and hence is grammatically incorrect as well. This eliminates option A.

A-D:

The tortuous talks on Brexit, which are now entering a critical stage, and marketing departments of the future cost of supplies in order to assist them in their forecasting.

The sentence above after combining the fragments doesn't make any sense.Hence,it is able to eliminate.

B-F:

Industrial purchasing may be defined as the decision-making process by which formal organizations establish the need for purchased products and services.

This complete sentence is evidently correct, both grammatically and contextually.
Hence, it makes only option **D** is correct option.

10. Let's use elimination technique to cancel the choices that are absurd or irrelevant.

C-D: Bihar is the remarkable state that gave two and one of the two headstreams of the Ganga.

The sentence above after combining the fragments doesn't make any sense.

C-E: Bihar is the remarkable state that gave two important religions – Buddhism and Jainism to the world.

The sentence after combining the fragments does make sense and is hence correct.

A-D: The Alaknanda is a Himalayan river in the Indian state of Uttarakhand and one of the two headstreams of the Ganga.

The sentence after combining the fragments does make sense and is hence correct.

A-F: The Alaknanda is a Himalayan river in the Indian state of Uttarakhand the fourth smallest by population.

The sentence above after combining the fragments doesn't make any sense.

B-F: Goa is India's smallest state by area and the the fourth smallest by population.
The sentence after combining the fragments does not make sense as there are two the's present in the sentence and is hence incorrect.
Clearly, option E is correct answer.

Sentence Connectors

Directions: You are required to match statements from columns 1 and 2 and find which of the following pairs of statement make sense meaningfully and grammatically.

1.

	Column (1)		Column (2)
(A)	The eagle was afraid to fly into the sky	(D)	in spite of the Internet has a plethora of options.
(B)	The shrewd businessman quickly	(E)	after remain in captivity for two years.
(C)	Freelancing has always been a popular way to earn money online	(F)	grabbed beneath the opportunity and earned a huge pile of money.

A. Only A-E and C-D
B. Only B-F and C-D
C. Only A-E and B-F
D. Only C-D
E. None of these

2.

	Column (1)		Column (2)
(A)	The audience gave the veteran musician	(D)	in the country today and covers over 50 per cent of Kerala households.
(B)	Kudumbashree is one of the largest women- empowerment projects	(E)	a standing ovation.
(C)	Children who have been victims of violence are more	(F)	likely to drop out of high school before graduation than their peers.

A. Only A-E
B. Only A-E and B-D
C. Only B-D and C-F
D. A-E, B-D and C-F
E. None of these

3.

	Column (1)		Column (2)
(A)	The tsunami swept over the island	(D)	will spur more Indian entrepreneurship.
(B)	The printer was out of ink and	(E)	hence showed promise of growth and vitality.
(C)	Hopefully the momentum at both PhonePe and Paytm	(F)	and destroyed over 2 billion dollars of property.

A. Only A-F
B. Only A-F and B-E
C. Only A-F and C-D
D. Only C-D
E. None of these

4.

	Column (1)		Column (2)
(A)	The angry mob	(D)	on the lines of defense public sector undertakings.
(B)	The Centre is considering converting the factories into multiple companies	(E)	beat upon the thief mercilessly.
(C)	The four indicators for the hunger index	(F)	are undernourishment, child stunting, child wasting and child mortality.

A. Only A-E B. Only B-D C. Only C-F
D. Only B-D and C-F E. None of these

5.

	Column (1)		Column (2)
(A)	My sister fought with two boys	(D)	his son failed to secure good marks of Mathematics.
(B)	The anguished cricketer lashed out	(E)	and won the surprise tests.
(C)	The father was deeply pained as	(F)	at the journalists when they went to ask him questions.

A. Only A-E B. Only B-F C. Only C-D
D. Only A-E and C-D E. None of these

6.

	Column (1)		Column (2)
(A)	It is high time we looked forward to	(D)	while it ceases to generate income for the lender.
(B)	An asset is tagged as non-performing	(E)	non-conventional and renewable energy sources like hydroelectricity, solar energy and wind energy.
(C)	Large number of rural people and students belonging to poorer sections of society	(F)	cannot avail to these benefits of internet and virtual education.

A. Only A-E B. Only B-D C. B-D and C-F
D. A-E and C-F E. None of these

7.

	Column (1)		Column (2)
(A)	Degraded into minuscule particles by the sun's ultraviolet rays,	(D)	should be introduced from all sectors of the Indian railways.
(B)	Modern advanced technologies and automatic signaling systems	(E)	the inimical environmental state of the union territory.
(C)	Noise pollution and water pollution add to	(F)	plastic is eaten by the fish and consequently through the food chain reaches all other marine animals.

A. Only A-F
B. A-F and B-D
C. Only C-E
D. A-F and C-E
E. None of these

8.

	Column (1)		Column (2)
(A)	Media holds an important position to sway public opinion and	(D)	that a man should by reason of birth, be denied or given extra privileges.
(B)	It is against the fundamental principles of humanity, it is against the dictates of reason	(E)	spread knowledge, awareness, and love rather than only using it as a tool of self-gratification.
(C)	Social media can serve as a great tool of the modern world if use it to	(F)	it ought to be responsibly enough to perform the noble mission of enlightening people.

A. Only A-F
B. A-F and B-D
C. Only B-D
D. B-D and C-E
E. None of these

9.

	Column (1)		Column (2)
(A)	Terrorists are often encouraged by countries with vested interests,	(D)	contributed a great deal to the issue of unemployment.
(B)	Gradual automation through artificial intelligence and robotics	(E)	with the aim of creating instability in a particular country or region.
(C)	Collective efforts, on the part of the policy-makers and the citizens, are necessary	(F)	to beget various socio-economic problems like increased crime rate, poverty and political instability.

A. Only A-E
B. Only B-D
C. A-E and B-D
D. A-E, B-D and C-F
E. None of these

3. **Checking A-F:**

The tsunami swept over the island and destroyed over 2 billion dollars of property.

The above sentence is correct both grammatically and contextually. Hence, the pair A-F is valid.

Checking B-E:

The printer was out of ink and hence showed promise of growth and vitality.

Contextually speaking, the above sentence does not make any sense. Hence, the pair B-E is invalid.

Checking C-D:

Hopefully the momentum at both PhonePe and Paytm will spur more Indian entrepreneurship.

The above sentence is correct both grammatically and contextually. Hence, the pair C-D is valid.

Hence option C is the correct answer.

4. **Checking A-E:**

The angry mob beat upon the thief mercilessly.

The sentence is grammatically erroneous. The correct preposition after 'beat' should have been 'up' instead of 'upon'. The pair A-E is hence invalid.

Checking B-D:

The Centre is considering converting the factories into multiple companies on the lines of defense public sector undertakings.

The above sentence is correct both grammatically and contextually. Hence, the pair B-D is valid.

Checking C-F:

The four indicators for the hunger index are undernourishment, child stunting, child wasting and child mortality.

The above sentence is correct both grammatically and contextually. Hence, the pair C-F is valid.

Hence, option D is the correct answer.

5. **Checking A-E:**

My sister fought with two boys and won the surprise tests.

The sentence does not make any sense contextually. The pair A-E is hence invalid.

Checking B-F:

The anguished cricketer lashed out at the journalists when they went to ask him questions.

The above sentence is correct both grammatically and contextually. Hence, the pair B-F is valid.

Checking C-D:

The father was deeply pained as his son failed to secure good marks of Mathematics.

The sentence does not make any sense grammatically. The correct preposition in front of "Mathematics" should have been 'in' instead of 'of'. The pair C-D is hence invalid.

Hence, option B is the correct answer.

6. **Checking A-E:**

It is high time we looked forward to non-conventional and renewable energy sources like hydroelectricity, solar energy and wind energy.

The above sentence is correct both grammatically and contextually.

Checking B-D:

An asset is tagged as non-performing while it ceases to generate income for the lender.

The usage of "while" is erroneous here. The word "when" would have been correct in place of "while" here. "While" denotes 'a period of time' which is incongruous here. Hence the pair B-D is invalid.

Checking C-F:

Large number of rural people and students belonging to poorer sections of society cannot avail to these benefits of internet and virtual education.

The usage of the preposition "to" is erroneous after avail. "Avail" never takes 'to' after it. In some instances, 'avail' may be followed by 'of'. Hence, the pair C-F is invalid.

Hence, option A is the correct answer.

7. **Checking A-F:**

Degraded into minuscule particles by the sun's ultraviolet rays, plastic is eaten by the fish and consequently through the food chain reaches all other marine animals.

The above sentence is correct both grammatically and contextually.

Checking B-D:

Modern advanced technologies and automatic signaling systems should be introduced from all sectors of the Indian railways.

The usage of "from" after introduced is erroneous. The correct preposition after introduced would have been 'in'. Hence the pair B-D is invalid.

Checking C-E:

Noise pollution and water pollution add to the inimical environmental state of the union territory.

The above sentence is correct both grammatically and contextually.

Hence, option D is the correct answer.

8. **Checking A-F:**

Media holds an important position to sway public opinion and it ought to be responsibly enough to perform the noble mission of enlightening people.

The usage of "responsibly" is erroneous in the given sentence. "Responsibly" is an adverb, but the the sentence demands an adjective in place of "responsibly". "Responsible" would have been correct in place of "responsibly". Hence, the pair A-F is invalid.

Checking B-D:

It is against the fundamental principles of humanity, it is against the dictates of reason that a man should by reason of birth, be denied or given extra privileges.

The above sentence is correct both grammatically and contextually.

Checking C-E:

Social media can serve as a great tool of the modern world if use it to spread knowledge, awareness, and love rather than only using it as a tool of self-gratification.

The above sentence is correct both grammatically and contextually.

Hence, option D is the correct answer.

9. **Checking A-E:**

Terrorists are often encouraged by countries with vested interests, with the aim of creating instability in a particular country or region.

The above sentence is correct both grammatically and contextually.

Checking B-D:

Gradual automation through artificial intelligence and robotics contributed a great deal to the issue of unemployment.

The above sentence is correct both grammatically and contextually.

Checking C-F:

Collective efforts, on the part of the policy-makers and the citizens, are necessary to beget various socio-economic problems like increased crime rate, poverty and political instability.

The sentence does not make any sentence. Part/column 1 does not fit with part/column 2. Policy-makers and citizens would never put in efforts to beget various socio-economic problems like increased crime rate, poverty and political instability. Hence, the pair C-F is invalid.

Hence, option C is the correct answer.

10. **Checking A-E:**
Yoga is not just a form of exercise that includes stretching and folding of body parts, but is much more than that.

The above sentence is correct both grammatically and contextually.

Checking B-F:
Personal laws, in many respects, encroach upon the fundamental rights of many, especially the women.

The above sentence is correct both grammatically and contextually.

Checking C-D:
The ones against the idea of UBI believe, the money will come from reduction in existing subsidies or from increase in indirect taxes.

The above sentence is correct both grammatically and contextually.

Hence, option E is the correct answer.

Direction: There are sets of four statements in question given below which, when connected using the correct sentence structure forms a complete single sentence without altering the meaning of the sentences given in the question. There are four options given below the question, choose the sentence that forms the correct formation of single sentence which is both grammatically correct and contextually meaningful. If none follows, choose (e) as your answer.

Questions:

1. When Uber and Lyft were voted out of Austin, Texas, for not agreeing to follow rules on background checks of their drivers, their drivers were left in the lurch; It was the city that helped them bounce back by organising job fairs; If the same were to occur in India, the number of affected drivers would be far greater; especially looking at the apathy towards taxi drivers as a class of urban workers.

A. When Uber and Lyft were voted out of Austin, Texas, for not agreeing to follow rules on background checks of their drivers as per the state's policy, their drivers were left in the lurch and It was the city that helped them bounce back by organising job fairs but if the same were to occur in India, the number of affected drivers would be far greater what with the apathy towards taxi drivers as a class of urban workers.

B. If the affected drivers would be far greater in India, it looks more apathetic and when Uber and Lyft were voted out of Austin, Texas, for not agreeing to follow rules on background checks of their drivers as per the state's policy, their drivers were left in the lurch and then they made the same happen in India, where there was more apathy.

C. The city that helped them bounce back by organising job fairs when they were left in the lurch and Uber and Lyft were voted out of Austin, Texas, for not agreeing to follow rules on background checks of their drivers as per the state's policy and also if the same were to occur in India, the number of affected drivers would be far greater what with the apathy towards taxi drivers as a class of urban workers.

D. Uber and Lyft were voted out of Austin, Texas because their drivers were left in the lurch for not agreeing to follow rules on background checks and it was the city that helped them bounce back by organising job fairs simultaneously if the same were to occur in India, the number of affected drivers would be far greater what with the apathy towards taxi drivers as a class of urban workers.

E. None of the above

2. Pakistan's general elections are scheduled to be held in July 2018; there is a popular argument that the Pakistani military has revived complete dominance and hegemony over civilian and electoral politics; however, fewer people are now buying into the opinion; many don't believe that the military is somehow "better" than democracy.

A. There is popular argument that the Pakistani military has revived complete dominance and hegemony over civilian and electoral politics and fewer people are now buying into the opinion in Pakistan that Pakistan's general elections are scheduled to be held in July 2018 and the military is somehow "better" than democracy.

B. Many don't believe that the military is somehow "better" than democracy and as Pakistan's general elections are scheduled to be held in July 2018 and there is a popular argument that the Pakistani military has revived complete dominance and hegemony over civilian and electoral politics.

C. Fewer people are buying the news that Pakistan's general elections are scheduled to be held in July 2018 and are popularly arguing that the Pakistani military has revived complete dominance and hegemony over civilian and electoral politics because many don't believe that the military is somehow "better" than democracy.

D. Pakistan's general elections are scheduled to be held in July 2018. Contrary to the popular argument that the Pakistani military has revived complete dominance and hegemony over civilian and electoral politics, fewer people are now buying into the opinion in Pakistan that the military is somehow "better" than democracy.

E. None of the above

3. The problems of implementation of a plastic ban are not unique to India; Across the world, there are multiple bans on plastic; There exists taxation of plastic bags; These have achieved mixed results; many of them have failed even in the developed world.

A. The problems of implementation of a plastic ban are not unique to India. Across the world, bans on plastic and taxation of plastic bags have achieved mixed results, with many of them failing even in the developed world.

B. Across the world, mixed results have been achieved due to bans on plastic and taxation of plastic bags after failing in the developed world and thus, this issue of problems of implementation is not unique to India.

C. With many of bans failing even in the developed world, across the world, there are bans on plastic and taxation of plastic bags which will be achieved mixed results with the problem of implementation of a plastic ban not be unique to India.

D. Having achieved mixed results in the developed world, the multiple bans on plastic and taxation on plastic bags have now found a calling in India but with problems of implementation that are not unique to India.

E. None of the above

4. The Prime Minister made an announcement on the World Environment Day; India would eliminate single-use plastics by 2022; this is a dramatic statement of intent; it is not yet evident that the deadline is based on a considered plan to make this actually happen.

A. Edicts and pronouncements do not bring about change and need to be backed by detailed, realistic, and implementable plans like India would eliminate single-use plastics by 2022 but is not yet evident that the deadline is based on a considered plan to make this actually happen.

B. It is not yet evident that the claim that India would eliminate single-use plastics by 2022 is a dramatic statement of intent and is based on a considered plan to make this actually happen as per an announcement on the World Environment Day made by the Prime Minister.

C. Although Prime Minister's announcement on 5 June, World Environment Day, that India would eliminate single-use plastics by 2022 is a dramatic statement of intent, it is not yet evident that the deadline is based on a considered plan to make this actually happen.

D. In a dramatic statement of intent made by the Prime Minister on the World Environment Day, what is not yet evident is the deadline that is basis on a considered plan to make this actually happen so as to eliminate single-use plastics by 2022.

E. None of the above

5. A press conference took place after Trump's meeting with Kim; Trump stated he hoped to bring the 32,000 US troops stationed in South Korea back home at some point; Trump agreed to stop the war games; War games refer to the US's joint military exercises with South Korea that repeatedly threatened North Korea with war.

A. Trump stated he hoped to bring the 32,000 US troops stationed in South Korea back home because at some point they agreed to stop the war games and refer to the US's joint military exercises with South Korea that repeatedly threatened North Korea with war when a press conference took place after Trump's meeting with Kim.

B. At the press conference after his meeting with Kim, Trump disclosed that he had agreed to stop the war games, that is, the US's joint military exercises with South Korea that repeatedly threatened North Korea with war and he also said that he hoped to bring the 32,000 US troops stationed in South Korea back home at some point.

C. War games are the US's joint military exercises with South Korea that repeatedly threaten North Korea with war but have been stopped by Trump, who also said that a press conference will take place after Trump's meeting with Kim in which he hoped to bring the 32,000 US troops stationed in South Korea.

D. Trump will agreed to stop the war games with South Korea to threaten North Korea with war and hold a press conference after Trump's meeting with Kim because he wanted to bring the 32,000 US troops stationed in South Korea back home at some point.

E. None of the above

6. The Pradhan Mantri Ujjwala Yojana completed two years of operation recently; the number of LPG connections has crossed 4 crore; Distributing new connections is no mean feat; the greater challenge for the mission lies in refills.

A. The number of LPG connections has crossed 4 crore because the Pradhan Mantri Ujjwala Yojana completed two years of operation recently and as the greater challenge for the mission lies in refills, distributing new connections is no mean feat.

B. As distributing new connections is no mean feat, the Pradhan Mantri Ujjwala Yojana completed two years of operation recently and number of LPG connections has crossed 4 crore with the greater challenge for the mission being in refills.

C. Recently the Pradhan Mantri Ujjwala Yojana completed two years of operation during which the number of LPG connections has crossed 4 crore but while distributing new connections is no mean feat, the greater challenge for the mission lies in refills.

D. The greater challenge for the Pradhan Mantri Ujjwala Yojana has been to complete two years of operation during which number of LPG connections has crossed 4 crore and distributing and refilling the connections is no mean feat.

E. None of the above

7. The collapse of the Ottoman Empire was a tectonic event; The Ottoman empire collapsed with the end of World War I; The collapse of the Ottoman Empire made possible the founding of the Turkish republic; The collapse of the Ottoman Empire empowered Ataturk to transform the Turkish society.

A. The collapse of the Ottoman Empire with the end of World War I was the tectonic event that had enabled the founding of the Turkish republic and empowered Atatürk to transform Turkish society.

B. The collapse of the Empire led to the End of the World War I which was tectonic and led to the founding of the Turkish republic and empowered Atatürk to transform Turkish society.

C. The World War I was a tectonic event that led to the collapse of the Ottoman Empire and also led to the founding of the Turkish republic which transformed the Turkish society by Ataturk.

D. The collapse of the Ottoman Empire empowered Ataturk to transform the Turkish society by making it a tectonic event which collapsed with the end of World War I and enabled the founding of the Turkish republic.

E. None of the above

8. The US Federal Reserve tightened its monetary policy; This caused the price of American debt to fall and yields to rise; This has pushed investors to invest in the U.S. where they can get higher returns; this has led to investors pulling money out of India and other emerging market economies.

A. The price of American debt has fallen and yields to rise as they pushed investors to invest in the U.S. where they can get higher returns by pulling money out of India and other emerging market economies because the US Federal Reserve tightened its monetary policy.

B. Investors have been pulling money out of India and other emerging market economies in the US Federal Reserve by tightened its monetary policy has caused them to invest in the U.S. where they can get higher returns by allowing American debt to fall and yields to rise.

C. Investors have been pushed by the US Federal Reserve to invest in the US where they can get returns that are lower than India and other emerging economies and they have been forced to pull out money from these economies because the price of American debt has fallen and yields have risen.

D. The tightening of monetary policy by the U.S. Federal Reserve has caused the price of American debt to fall and yields to rise which in turn has pushed investors to pull money out of India and other emerging market economies in order to invest in the U.S. where they can get higher returns.

E. None of the above

9. There has been inadequate government funding since independence; Building a mass higher education system with inadequate government funding has been a challenge; this inadequate funding has led to poor quality, increasing privatisation and politicization; There are indications of things changing at the Central government level in the past several years.

A. Since Independence, the challenges of building a mass higher education system with inadequate government funding has meant poor quality, increasing privatisation and politicization but in the past several years, there are indications that things are changing at the Central government level.

B. Building a mass higher education system has been a challenge and this has led to poor quality, increasing privatisation and politicization as well as inadequate government funding but now there are indications of things changing at the Central government level in the past several years.

C. With indications in the past several years of things changing at the Central government level, there has been inadequate government funding since independence which has led to a mass higher education system with quality, increasing privatisation and politicization.

D. Both A and C

E. None of the above

10. Recently the World Health Organisation declared 14 Indian cities as among the most polluted in the world; surprisingly the government is looking at sourcing untested technologies; this includes the production of 2G ethanol; The government is silent on octane which has direct consequences on vehicular emissions thereby affecting air pollution.

A. Even though the government is silent on octane which has direct consequences on vehicular emissions thereby affecting air pollution, it is looking at sourcing untested technologies like the production of 2G ethanol and so when the World Health Organisation has already declared 14 Indian cities as among the most polluted in the world.

B. At a time when the World Health Organisation has declared 14 Indian cities as among the most polluted in the world, it is surprising that the government is looking at sourcing untested technologies like the production of 2G ethanol and is totally silent on octane, which has direct consequences on vehicular emissions thereby affecting air pollution.

C. Including the production of 2G ethanol, the government is looking at sourcing untested technologies because recently the World Health Organisation declared 14 Indian cities as among the most polluted in the world for the government is silent on octane which has direct consequences on vehicular emissions thereby affecting air pollution.

D. Recently the World Health Organisation declared 14 Indian cities as among the most polluted in the world because the government is looking at sourcing untested technologies as it is silent on octane which has direct consequences on vehicular emissions thereby affecting air pollution.

E. None of the above

Correct Answers:

1	2	3	4	5	6	7	8	9	10
A	D	A	C	B	C	A	D	A	B

Explanations:

1. Option B is incorrect as the statement is totally incorrect and conveys a different meaning than that stated in the original set.

Option C is incorrect as the pronouns 'they' and 'them' mentioned in the beginning have not been specified before and the statement so formed is meaningless.

Option D changes the meaning of the statement by stating that the drivers did not agree for a background check which is incorrect and then they moved to India, which is absurd.

Option A is correct and states everything right grammatically as well as contextually.

Hence, option A is the correct answer.

2. Option A is incorrect as this changes the meaning of the original set and seems to imply that there are less number of people believing in the fact that elections are to be held in July.

Option B is incorrect as the statement seems to imply that there are arguments about when the Pakistan elections would be held while in the original set, this is a given fact and not an opinion. This changes the meaning of the set and is incorrect.

Option C is incorrect for the same reason stated for option B.

Option D is correct and states everything right grammatically as well as contextually.

Hence, option D is the correct answer.

3. Option B is incorrect as it seems to imply that the bans were imposed on plastics after they failed in the developed nations which is not the case as per the original set.

Option C is incorrect as it is not meaningful in terms of structure and grammar.

Option D is incorrect as it changes the entire meaning of the original set and seems to imply that fater failing in the developed nations, Its implementation has been successful in India with some problems being common to the other nations.

Option A is correct and states everything right grammatically as well as contextually.
Hence, option A is the correct answer.

4. Statement A is incorrect as the first few fragments of the line are not a part of the original set and cannot be included as such.

Option B is incorrect as it seems to say that the claim of India eliminating single-use plastic is not dramatic. This is opposite of what the original set states.

Option D is incorrect as the sentence structure is incorrect as the *statement of intent* is to be elaborated in the beginning and not the end. Also, the use of the word *basis* is incorrect and should be replaced with *based.*

Statement C is correct and states everything right grammatically as well as contextually.

Hence, option C is the correct answer.

5. Statement A is incorrect as it simply does not make a meaningful statement on reading.

Statement C is incorrect as in the original set, Trump has merely agreed to stop the War games and has not already stopped them. Also, he did not say that the press conference would take place after his meeting with Kim.

Statement D is incorrect as the phrase 'will agreed' is incorrect in terms of tense usage. Also, the statement here implies that stopping the war games will threaten North Korea while the opposite is true.

Statement B is correct and states everything right grammatically as well as contextually.

Hence, option B is the correct answer.

6. The first option is incorrect as it creates a cause and effect relationship between the number of connections and the scheme completing 2 years. Also, the relationship established between refills and new distribution is incorrect.

Option B is incorrect as it creates an incorrect relationship between giving out new connections and PMUY and in general the sentence structure is also incorrect.

Option D is incorrect as it implies the PMUY found it tough to complete 2 years.

Option C is correct contextually and grammatically. It links all the statements in the correct way.

Hence, option C is correct.

7. Option B is absurd as it implies that the collapse of the Ottomans led to ending of the WWI.

Option C is incorrect as it implies the ending of WWI led to collapse of the Ottoman Empire.

Option D implies the collapse of the Ottoman Empire transformed the Turkish society by making it a tectonic event. This is absurd and meaningless.

Option A is correct contextually and grammatically. It links all the statements in the correct way.

Hence, option A is correct.

8. Option A is incorrect as it is grammatically absurd and the statement also does not make sense in terms of structure.

Option B is incorrect as the phrase 'economies in the US Federal Reserve' is incorrect. Also, it implies that the investors decide when bond yields fall or rise which is absurd.

Option C is incorrect as it implies the US Fed has forced them to invest in the US where the returns are *lower*. This is factually incorrect from the original set of statements.

Option D is correct contextually and grammatically. It links all the statements in the correct way.

Hence, option D is correct.

9. Option B is incorrect as it implies building the mass higher education system has led to inadequate funding.

Option C is incorrect as it implies that because things are changing at the central level, there has been inadequate funding.

Option A is correct contextually and grammatically. It links all the statements in the correct way.

Hence, option A is correct.

10. Option A is incorrect as it implies sourcing untested technologies like the production of 2G ethanol is a good thing while it is the opposite in the original set.

Option C is incorrect as it implies that because the WHO listed Indian cities as the most polluting, India is introducing untested technologies.

Option D is incorrect as it implies the WHO listed Indian cities as polluted due to India sourcing untested technologies which is incorrect.

Option B is correct contextually and grammatically. It links all the statements in the correct way.

Hence, option B is correct.

Direction: In each of the following questions, two statements and five connectors are given. Only one of the connectors from those given can be used to combine the given two statements into one sentence without changing the meaning. Choose that connector as your answer.

1. I. The school has the best research infrastructure in the town.

II. The students are not at all interested in pursuing education.

A. Owing to B. Hence C. Because of D. However E. None of the above

2. I. I didn't want to get into the depth of the matter at any cost.

II. I took the book from the shelf and started reading with great attention.

A. Instead B. In contrast C. On the other hand D. However E. None of the above

3. I. I am of the opinion that there is no problem with his technique to play the short ball.

II. I will talk to him about this the first thing after the match today.

A. Nonetheless B. Because C. Hence D. By comparison E. None of the above

4. I. The monsoon has been very late this year and it has only started raining now.

II. The farmers are demanding compensation from the government for their revenue loss.

A. Nevertheless B. Though C. Owing to D. Yet E. None of the above

5. I. The team played its heart out in the match.

II. The result had nothing to show for the efforts put into the match by them.

A. Nonetheless B. Since C. As D. Because E. None of the above

6. **I. The office has got the best staff in the town for this job.**

II. The higher management is not at all interested in its development.

A. By virtue of B. By comparison C. On the contrary D. However E. None of the above

7. **I. Utility employees should not be made to resign from the company at any cost.**

II. In the long run the company is bound to suffer.

A. Nevertheless B. Otherwise C. In any case D. Instead E. None of the above

8. **I. The notification by the Reserve Bank of India to do away with stapling of currency notes by banks has not done much difference.**

II. Banks are left with no other option but to issue the old notes to their customers in the absence of fresh notes from the RBI.

A. Due to B. Because of C. As D. Hence E. None of the above

9. **I. I am of the opinion that my father would have done it the same way had he known this fact.**

II. The differences we had when he was alive.

A.Due to B. Instead of C. Because of D. As E. Since

10. **I. The popularity of cricket eating into the share of revenue of other sports in India for many years now.**

II. All other sports are suffering and India is not able to win medals in Olympics in all such sports.

A. Because of B. Therefore C. Henceforth D. Due to E. None of the above

Correct Answers:

1	2	3	4	5	6	7	8	9	10
D	A	A	C	A	D	B	C	B	D

Explanations:

1. Here the two statements have been used in the sense that the school has the best infrastructure for conducting research but the students are not at all interested in taking advantage of that. Only however can be used to connect these two sentences since the first one is about some facility whereas the next is about how that is going in vain. All the other connectors are used to connect sentences that have cause and effect relationship between them. So, all of them can be eliminated. The connected sentence would be: The school has the best research infrastructure in the town, **however,** the students are not at all interested in pursuing education.
This makes Option D the correct choice among the given options.

2. If we take into account the context of the two given statements, it is regarding the fact that I did not want to listen to the matter and started reading the book. In contrast is not correct because it is used to indicate something that is opposite to the other and it is certainly not fit in the given context. On the other hand and however can also be eliminated since they cannot connect these two given statements. Only instead can be used in order to connect the two sentences without changing the meaning.

The connected statement would be: I didn't want to get into the depth of the matter at any cost, **instead,** I took the book from the shelf and started reading with great attention.

This makes Option A the correct choice among the given options.

3. The two statements are regarding the context that the person does not think that there is no problem with his technique to play the short ball but he will definitely talk about it with him after the match. Among the given connectors, both because and hence are mainly used for statements that have cause and effect relationship whereas by comparison is used in order to indicate any kind of comparison. Only nonetheless can connect these two statements since it implies in spite of that and that is why it can be used to connect these two statements without changing the meaning.

The connected sentence would be: I am of the opinion that there is no problem with his technique to play the short ball, **nonetheless,** I will talk to him about this the first thing after the match today.

This makes Option A the correct choice among the given options.

4. Here the given two statements carry a cause and effect relationship. The reason the farmers are asking for compensation is because of the late onset of monsoon in the country. That is the main reason the farmers have lost their revenue. Among the given connectors, we can see that nevertheless can be used to indicate that in spite of something we have done something else whereas though and yet are also not correct here. There is only one connector that can be used here i.e. owing to.

The connected sentence would be: **Owing to** the late monsoon and rains this year, the farmers are demanding compensation from the government for their revenue loss.

This makes Option C the correct choice among the given options.

5. According to the given context we can see that the players in the team played very well but at the end of the day they lost of the match. Therefore nothing could be shown against the efforts put forward by the players in the match. Nonetheless is used to imply in spite of whereas the rest of the three connectors are mainly used for the purpose of connecting the cause and effect related sentences.

The connected sentence would be:

The team played its heart out in the match, **nonetheless,** the result had nothing to show for the efforts put into the match by them.

This makes Option A the correct choice among the given options.

6. It can be understood that the two sentences can be connected in order to imply that the office can do well but the management is not that interested to pursue the same. That is why in spite of having good and dedicated staff under its belt, it has failed to produce wonderful results. Among the given connecting words, we can use however in order to connect the sentences without changing the meaning. By virtue of means because of something, by comparison implies comparing something whereas on the contrary refers to being the opposite of something.

The connected sentence would be:

The office has got the best staff in the town for this job, **however**, the higher management is not at all interested in its development.

This makes Option D the correct choice among the given options.

7. Here we are talking about the fact that if the employees are not made to stay back it is bound that the organization will suffer in the long run. Therefore the relation is regarding the cause and effect here. Nevertheless implies in spite of something whereas instead is used to connect sentences that have the relation regarding in place of something.

The connected sentence would be:

Utility employees should not be made to resign from the company at any cost, **otherwise,** in the long run the company is bound to suffer.

This makes Option B the correct choice among the given options.

8. If we read the two sentences they are connected by the cause and effect relationship where one is the reason and the other is the result of something. Among the given options, 'as' is the correct choice since it connects the sentences as cause and effect.

Combining the two sentences the new sentence will be:

As banks are left with no other option but to issue the old notes to their customers in the absence of fresh notes from the RBI, the notification by the Reserve Bank of India to do away with stapling off currency notes by banks has not done much difference.

So, Option C is the right choice among the given options.

9. Exp: If we read the sentences it is clear that it talks about two contrasting things. Among the given choices, 'instead of' is the right fit as it means that 'despite the fact that'.

Combing the two sentences the new statement will be:

Instead of the differences we had when he was alive, I am of the opinion that my father would have done it the same way had he known this fact.

So, Option B is the right choice.

10. Exp: If we read the two sentences, we shall observe that they are connected by the cause and effect relationship. Hence, ‘due to’ will be the perfect fit in the given context as it means that ‘for this reason’.

Combing the two sentences the new sentence will be:

Due to the popularity of cricket eating into the share of revenue of other sports in India for many years now, all other sports are suffering and India is not able to win medals in Olympics in all such sports.

So, Option D is the correct choice among the given options.

IDIOMS AND PHRASES

IDIOMS AND PHRASES

Idioms and Phrases form an important part of the English section of various competitive exams such as SSC exams, RRB exams, Bank exams and other Government exams. Candidates can easily fetch a good score in the English section if they are aware of important idioms and phrases, along with their meanings.

Idioms & Phrases	Meanings
Rank and File	Ordinary People
By fits and starts	In short periods, not regularly
A wee bit	A little
Out of the wood	Free from difficulties and dangers
Under his thumb	Under his control
At one's wits end	In a state where one does not know what to do
Between the devil and the deep sea	Between two dangers
Burn the midnight oil	Work or study hard
Call a spade a spade	Speak frankly and directly
Come off with flying colors	Be highly successful
Hoping against hope	Without hope
Hit the nail on the head	Do or say the exact thing
An axe to grind	A personal interest in the matter
To get rid of	Dispose of
At daggers drawn	Bitterly hostile

To play ducks and drakes	To act foolishly or inconsistently
To take the bull by the horns	To tackle a problem in a bold and direct fashion
Rain cats and dogs	Rain heavily
To move heaven and earth	To make a supreme effort
No avail	Without any result
Bark up the wrong tree	Accuse or denounce the wrong person
Keep one at bay	Keep one at a distance
Make a clean breast of it	Confess – especially when a person has done a wrong thing
Have a card up one's sleeve	Have a secret plan in reserve
Like a cat on hot bricks	Very nervous
Cat and dog life	Life full of quarrels
Cock and bull story	Made up story that one should not believe
Cry for the moon	Ask for the impossible
The pros and cons	The various aspects of a matter in detail
Be in a tight corner	In a very difficult situation
Cross one's t's and dot	Be precise, careful and one's i's exact
At arm's length	To keep at a distance
Out of the question	Impossible
Out of the way	Strange
Show a clean pair of heals	Run away
Keep one's fingers crossed	The anxiety in which you hope that nothing will upset your plans

Sitting on the fence	Hesitate between two decisions
Spread like wild fire	Spread quickly
The gift of the gab	Talent for speaking
By hook or by crook	By fair or foul means
Feather one's own nest	Make money unfairly
Throw out of gear	Disturb the work
Take to one's heels	Run away
Tooth and nail	With all one's power
Die in harness	Die while in service
Take a leaf out of one's book	Imitate one
Leave no stone unturned	Use all available means
A man of straw	A man of no substance
Read between the lines	Understand the hidden meaning
In cold blood	Deliberately and without emotion
A thorn in the flesh	A constant source of annoyance
Smell a rat	Suspect something foul
Harp on the same string	Dwell on the same subject
Bury the hatchet	End the quarrel and make peace
Leave one in the lurch	Desert one in difficulties; leave one in a helpless condition
Like a fish out of water	In a strange situation

At one's beck and call	Under his control
To make both ends meet	To live within one's income
In hot water	In trouble
Nip in the bud	Destroy in the early stage
Stick to one's guns	Remain faithful to the cause
To eat humble pie	To apologize humbly and to yield under humiliating circumstances
In high spirits	Very happy
Put the cart before the horse	Put or do things in the wrong order
To all names	To abuse
On tenterhooks	In a state of suspense and anxiety
Wash one's dirty linen	Discuss unpleasant in public-private matters before strangers
To bell the cat	To face the risk
A hard nut to crack	A difficult problem
Let the cat out of the bag	Reveal a secret
A big gun	An important person
Kill two birds with one stone	To achieve two results with one effort
Take one to task	Rebuke
Gain ground	Become Popular
To blow one's own	To praise one's own trumpet achievement
A bosom friend	A very close friend

A brown study	Dreaming
Turn a deaf ear	Disregard / ignore what one says
A close shave	Narrow escape
Turn over a new leaf	Change for the better
Make up one's mind	Decide
In the long run	Eventually; ultimately
Bring to light	Disclose
Pay off old scores	Take revenge
Hard and fast rules	Strict rules
At the eleventh hour	At the last moment
To cut a sorry figure	To make a poor show
With a high hand	Oppressively
Burn one's fingers	Get into trouble by interfering in other's affairs
Laugh one's head off	Laugh heartily
Chew the cud	Ponder over something
Play second fiddle	Take an unimportant part
Above board	Honest and open
Through thick and thin	Under all conditions
Put a spoke in one's wheel	To upset one's plans
At sixes and sevens	In a disordered/disorganized manner, chaotic

At home	Comfortable
Alpha and omega	The beginning and the end
At sea	Confused and lost
By leaps and bounds	Rapidly
To burn one's boats	Go back on a decision
To beat about the bush	Talk irrelevantly
To burn candle at both ends	To waste lavishly
A bone of contention	A source of quarrel
Add fuel to the fire	To aggravate the situation
An acid test	A critical test
At a snail's pace	Very slowly
A bolt from the blue	Something unexpected
To build castles in the air	Make imaginary schemes
Once in a blue moon	Something that happens very rarely
Beating around the bush	Avoiding the main topic
Cry over spilled milk	Complaining about a loss or failure from the past
Chip on your shoulder	When someone is upset about something that happened a while ago
Piece of cake	Something that is easy to understand or do
Golden handshake	A big sum of money given to a person when he/she leaves a companyor retires
Spill the beans	To disclose a secret

Blessing in disguise	Something good and useful that did not initially seem that way
Mean business	Being Serious or Dedicated
Come hell or high water	Possible obstacles in your path
Apple of one's eye	Being cherished
Bite off more than you can chew	Not able to complete a task due to lack of ability
The best of both worlds	The benefits of widely differing situations, enjoyed at the same time
Feeling a bit under the weather	Feeling slightly ill
Icing on the cake	Something that turns good into great
Cost an arm and a leg	Be very expensive
Jump the bandwagon	To join a popular activity or trend
Ball is in your court	When it is up to you to make the next decision or step
To be in the doldrums	To be in low spirits
To sit on the fence	To remain neutral
Break the ice	To initiate a social conversation or interaction
Hear it on grapevine	To hear rumors about something or someone
Can't judge a book by its cover	Cannot judge something primarily on appearance
It takes two to tango	Actions or communications need more than one person
Black and blue	Full of Bruises
Be on cloud nine	Be very happy
Last straw	The final problem in a series of problems

A bird's eye view	A view from a very high place that allows you to see a very large area
A litmus Test	A method that helps to know if something is correct
At the drop of a hat	Willingness to do something instantly
Afraid of one's own shadow	To become easily frightened
A house of cards	A poor plan
Fool's paradise	False sense of happiness
Get a raw deal	To not be treated as well as other people
Give cold shoulder	To ignore
Hand to mouth	Live on only basic necessities
Make a face	To show dislike or disappointment through facial expressions
It's Greek to me	Something that is not understandable
To pour oil on troubled waters	To make peace
Don't put all your eggs in one basket	Do not put all your resources in one basket (in one place or thing)
To put in a nutshell	To say in a few words or to make something concise
Back out	To withdraw from a promise or contract
Blow up	To explode
Back Up	To support and sustain
Back Upon	To be relevant
Break Down	Failure in something
Break off	To end or discontinue

Break Up	To disperse / dissolve
Bring up	To rear
Call forth	To provoke
Call out	To shout
Call upon	To order
Carry on	To continue
Cast away	To throw aside
Catch up with	To overtake
Come off	To take place
Cry Down	To make little of
Cry out against	To complain loudly against
Cut out	Designed for
Drop in	To Visit Casually
Drop out	To fall
Fall back	To Recede; To Retreat
Fall down	From a higher position to a lower one
Fall off	To Withdraw; To Drop Off
Fall under	To come under
Get along	To Prosper; To Progress; To Proceed
Get on with	To Live Pleasantly Together; To Progress

Get into	To be involved in
Give in	To Surrender; To Yield
Give over	Not to do any longer
Go after	To Follow; To Pursue
Go Down	To be accepted
Go without	To remain without
Go by	To follow
Hang about	To Loiter near a place
Hang upon	To depend upon
Hold out	To Endure; To Refuse to yield; To continue; To offer
Hold to	Abide By
Keep off	To ward off
Keep up with	To keep pace with
Knock out	To win by hitting another one
Keep something at bay	Keep something away
Let sleeping dogs lie	Leave something alone if it might cause trouble
Open the floodgates	Release something that was previously under control
Out of the blue	Happen unexpectedly
Out on a limb	Do something risky
Over the Top	Totally excessive and not suitable for the occasion

Pen is mightier than the sword	Words and communication have a greater effect than war
Push one's luck	Trying to obtain more than what one has
Reap the harvest	Benefit or suffer as a direct result of past actions
Roll up sleeves	To get yourself prepared
See eye to eye	To be in agreement with
Shot in the dark	A complete guess
Sink your teeth into	Do something with a lot of energy and enthusiasm
Take with a grain/pinch of salt	To doubt the accuracy of information
Skating on thin ice	Do or say something risky
Tight spot	A difficult situation
Strike while the iron is hot	To act at the right time
Take the plunge	Venture into something of one's interest despite the risks involved
Take a nosedive	Rapid drop or decrease in value
Think the world of	Admire someone very much
Stand in a good stead	To be useful or be of good service to someone
Take a back seat	Choose to be less important in a role
Wave a dead chicken	Do something useless
Whale of a time	Enjoy a lot
Wrap one's brain around	Concentrate on something to understand
Zero in on something	Focus all attention on one thing
Above all	Chiefly, Mainly

On Account of	Due to
On no account	Not for Any Reason
A Fidus Achates	A faithful friend or a devoted follower
The Heel of Achilles	A Weak Point
An Adonis	A very handsome man
To assume airs	To affect superiority
To stand aloof	To keep to oneself and not mix with others
To lead to the altar	To marry
An Ananias	A Liar
An Apollo	A Man with Perfect Physique
To Upset the Apple Cart	To disturb the peace
Apple Pie Order	In perfect order
Arcadian Life	A blissful, happy, rural and simple life
To take up arms	To fight or go to the war
To Grind	To have some selfish objective in view
To break the back of anything	To perform the most difficult part
To backbite a person	To speak disguise about someone
He has no backbone	He has no will of his own
To cause bad blood	To Cause Enmity
Bag and Baggage	With all one's belongings
To keep the ball rolling	To keep things going
Barmecide feast	Imaginary Benefits

Bee-line	The shortest distance between two places
Behind one's back	Without one's Knowledge
Behind the scenes	In Private
To hit below the belt	To act unfairly in a contest
To bite the dust	To be Defeated in Battle
A Wet Blanket	A person who discourages enjoyment or enthusiasm
A blue Stocking	A learned/educated or intellectual woman
At First Blush	At first sight
One's bread and butter	One's means of livelihood
To breathe one's last	To Die
To make bricks without straw	To attempt to do something without proper materials
To kick the bucket	To die
Good wine needs no bush	There is no need to advertise something good
To burn the candle at both ends	To expend energy in two directions at the same time
If the cap fits, wear it	If you think the remarks refer to you, then accept the criticism
Care killed the cat	Don't fret and worry yourself to death
To Catch one's eye	To attract attention
To take the chair	To preside a meeting
She is no chicken	She is older than she says
To pick and choose	To make a careful selection
To square the circle	To attempt something impossible
Every cloud has a silver lining	Adverse conditions do not last forever

Close fisted	Mean
Cut your cloth according to your cloth	Live within your income
A cock and bull story	A foolishly incredible story
To be cock sure	To be perfectly sure or certain
To throw cold water upon anything	To discourage efforts
Off color	Not in the usual form
To commit to memory	To learn by heart
Too many cooks spoil the broth	Where there are more workers than necessary
Crocodile tears	Hypocritical Tears
Cut and dried	Readymade
Up to date	Recent
Evil days	A period of misfortune
Halcyon Days	A time when there are peace and happiness in the land
To step into dead man's shoes	To come into an inheritance
Go to the devil	Be off
Devil's bones	Dice
Devil's Playthings	Playing Cards
Give a dog a bad name and hang him	Once a person loses his reputation
Every dog has his day	Sooner or later, everyone has his share of good fortune
To throw dust in one's eyes	To try to deceive someone or mislead someone
A white elephant	A useless possession which is extremely expensive to keep

To set the Thames on fire	To do something sensational or remarkable
A burnt child dreads the fire	One who has had a previous unpleasant experience is always scared ofsituations where such experiences are likely to be repeated
A fish out of water	Anyone in an awkward
Foul play	Cheating
To jump from a frying pan into fire	To come out of one trouble and get into a worse
All that glitters are not gold	Things are not always as attractive as they appear
To die in harness	To continue at one's occupation until death
Make hay while the sun shines	Take advantage of all opportunities
Lock, stock and barrel	The whole of everything
A miss is as good as a mile	Comes nowhere near it. If someone narrowly misses the target it still istreated as a missed one or failure.
One swallow does not makea summer	It is unreliable to base one's conclusions on only a single test or incident
If wishes were horses, beggars might ride	If wishing could make things happen, then even the most destitutepeople would have everything they wanted
A nine days' wonder	An event which relates a sensation for a time but is soon forgotten
Yellow press	Newspapers which publish sensational and unscrupulous stories andexaggerate the news to attract readers.
A ball park figure	A general financial figure
To balance the books	To make certain that the amount of money spent is not more than theamount of money received.
A cash cow	A product or service that makes a lot of money for a company
Devil's Advocate	To present a counter argument
Don't give up the day job	You are not very good at something. You could not do it professionally.
To cook the books	To modify financial statements
To get the sack	To be dismissed from your job

To be snowed under	To be very busy
To work your fingers to the bone / to sweat blood	To work really hard
Hear it on the grapevine	To hear rumors
In the heat of the moment	Overwhelmed by what is happening in the moment
Not a spark of decency	No Manners
Speak of the devil!	This expression is used when the person you have just been talkingabout arrives
Whole nine yards	Everything. All of it
Your guess is as good as mine	To have no idea about anything
Fishy	Doubtful, Suspicious
First and foremost	Extreme enthusiasm
Fire and fury	Fearful penalties
Fire and brimstone	A very tasty food or meal
Finding your feet/ Finger licking good	To become more comfortable in whatever you are doing
Fabian policy	Policy of delaying decisions
Excuse my French	Please forgive me for cussing
Everything but the kitchen sink	Almost everything and anything has been included
Break a leg	A superstitious way to say 'Good Luck' without saying 'Good Luck'
Barking up the wrong tree	A mistake made in something you are trying to achieve
Bated breath	In anxiety, expectancy
Beat a dead horse	To force an issue that has already ended
Between Scylla and Charybdis	Choice between two unpleasant alternatives

Directions (1-10): In each of the following questions a statement has been given with highlighted text. You are required to replace the text with correct Idioms or phrases given in the options.

1. At the drop of the hat:

a. As soon as it was spoken

b. Done easily, without any preparation

c. Done in an instant

d. After something is done

e. None of these

ANSWER: b. Done easily, without any preparation.

2. Keep at bay:

a. Keep at a distance

b. Keep at the sea-shore

c. Keep in mind

d. Keep thinking about something

e. None of these

ANSWER: a. Keep at a distance

3. A man of straw:

a. A man with no means

b. A generous man

c. A man of character

d. A man of no substance

e. None of these

ANSWER: d. A man of no substance

4. Give cold shoulder:

a. Shiver

b. Cold meat

c. To ignore

d. To support

e. None of these

ANSWER: c. To ignore

5. Hold one's horse:

a. Keep one's expectations

b. Keep one's gift

c. Have patience

d. High on energy

e. None of these

ANSWER: c. Have patience

6. Hornet's nest:

a. A bee's house

b. A violent situation

c. A busy house

d. A dangerous place

e. None of these

ANSWER: b. A violent situation

7. Never-never land

a. An ideal pace

b. Dream land

c. A worthless place

d. A useless situation

e. None of these

ANSWER: a. An ideal pace

8. Cap it all:

a. To cover everything
b. To seize everything
c. To finish
d. To occur
e. None of these

ANSWER: c. To finish

9. Like a sitting duck:

a. Lazy
b. Fat
c. Sleepy
d. Ignorant
e. crazy

ANSWER: d. Ignorant

10. Pull your socks up

a. To get ready
b. To improve
c. To start
d. To finish
e. None of these

ANSWER: b. To improve

11. To eat away:

a. Finish

b. Corrode

c. Destroy

d. Eat up

e. None of these

ANSWER: b. Corrode

12. To grow upon:

a. To grow

b. Nurture

c. Get a stronger hold on something gradually

d. To flourish

e. None of these

13. Long for:

a. Desire

b. Long

c. Far

d. Age

e. Small

ANSWER: a. Desire

14. To be well off:

a. Quite far away

b. To be in comfortable circumstances

c. Distant

d. Unrelated

e. None of these

ANSWER: b. To be in comfortable circumstances

15. Bore away:

a. Dug up

b. Get bored

c. Won

d. Passed time

e. None of these

ANSWER: c. Won

16. Get the better of:

a. Advantage over

b. Be better off

c. Take the better things and leave the rest

d. Take advantage of

e. None of these

ANSWER: a. Advantage over

17. Hear someone out:

a. Hear from far away

b. Dismiss someone

c. Keep someone out

d. Let someone complete what they are saying

e. None of these

ANSWER: d. Let someone complete what they are saying

18. Trump up:

a. Encourage

b. Fabricate

c. Trump card

d. Break
E. None of these

ANSWER: b. Fabricate

19. Break with:

a. Break

b. Interval

c. Relieve

d. Quarrel

e. Down

ANSWER: d. Quarrel

20. Put by:

a. Keep

b. Kill

c. Save

d. Set

e. Slap

ANSWER: c. Save

21. Dance to someone's tune

a. Argue with others on petty matters

b. Delay in making a decision

c. Do what others want you to do

d. Be engaged in an energetic activity

e. None of these

ANSWER: (C) Do what others want you to do

22. Leave no stone unturned

a. Try everything possible

b. Leave the path halfway

c. Not make enough efforts

d. Turn everything upside down

e. None of these

ANSWER: (A) Try everything possible

23. Throw in the towel

a. Think of a solution

b. Face the situation

c. Drop something

d. Admit defeat

e. None of these

ANSWER: (D) Admit defeat

24. To air dirty linen in public

a. To hang out clothes in the open

b. To stand up and fight

c. To discuss private affairs in public

d. To continue to complain

e. None of these

ANSWER: (C) To discuss private affairs in public

25. Tit for tat

a. To reward people for the good done

b. To do harm as done to you

c. To make someone angry

d. To take advantage of someone

e. None of these

ANSWER: (B) To do harm as done to you.

CLOZE TESTS

CLOZE TEST

Read Thoroughly

- Read the passage provided very thoroughly to form an idea about the topic.
- Read slowly and gain an understanding of the text.
- Once the theme of the text is somewhat clear, your job becomes easier.
- You can then go on to think of the appropriate words that suit the situation being described and proceed to filling in the blanks.

Link the Sentences Together

- Remember that it is a passage with sentences that are connected to each other.
- Do not make the mistake of treating each sentence like an individual one and filling in the blanks accordingly.
- Try to come up with logical connections that link up the sentences together and your job will automatically become easier.

The Type of Word to Fill in

- Now look at the blanks carefully and assess the kind of words you have to fill in.
- Which part of speech would it be? Would it be a noun, a pronoun, a verb, a preposition, a conjunction or an article?

For example:

A noun – I forgot to carry my ______ to school. I therefore had to share with my friend.
The logical answer here would be a book or tiffin.

An article – He ate ______ papaya and threw________ seeds away.
Articles are usually the easiest to answer. Fill in 'a' and 'an' where talking about general facts and 'the' when using it before something specific.

Here, the answer is 'the' or 'his' in the first case and 'the' or 'its' in the second.

A verb – ________for half an hour left me breathless.
The idea of being breathless connotes something strenuous like 'exercising' or 'running'. In this way, think of the appropriate word to fill in.

Eliminate Options

- We can easily identify most unfit/illogical words in answer options.
- We should quickly eliminate these words. Only after that we should try to most fit word. Elimination will enhance accuracy and hence score.

Go with Frequently Used Words

Sometimes, you may not be able to decide between two words. In this case, if you see a word in the options that is frequently used with the words around the blank, then pick that option.

For example

Can I have a _______ word with you?

A. Swift
B. Quick
C. Prompt

You can see that the three options nearly mean the same thing. How do you decide which one fits the blank?

Sometimes in English, some words are used more frequently with some others. Like 'bad habit', 'hardly ever', 'happy ending', 'take a seat', 'make room' etc. In the same way, the words 'quick' and 'word' are used together frequently. So 'quick' should be your answer in this case.

Check Tone of Passage

- The passage is usually written in a certain tone; sometimes narrative, sometimes critical, sometimes humorous.
- Pick words that fit in with the tone of the passage.

For example:

Jonah _______ down the stairs, bumping along like a quarter in a tumbling dryer.

A. tumbled
B. fell
C. dropped

Clearly, you can use either 'tumbled' or 'fell' in this blank. But the rest of the sentence is written in a humorous vein. So we try to maintain the tone of the sentence. This is best accomplished by the use of the word 'tumbled' as it brings to mind images of people falling funnily.

Practice More

- In the end, there is no substitute for hard work and practice.
- Try to complete three to four passages each day while preparing and get an insight into your problem areas.
- Work on them and go deliver your best

Helpful Hints

#1 You must ensure that the word you have inserted in the blank enables you to read the sentence smoothly and correctly

#2 Apply grammar rules (grammar rules – prepositions, noun, pronoun, adj, verb etc)

- **Preposition following a noun, adjective or verb. (Example: look at images)**
- **A prepositional phrase. (Example: in spite of)**
- **An adverb. (Example: they vacated the house two years ago)**
- **A connector. (Example: it is raining, therefore ground is wet.)**
- **A conjunction. (Example: although he is seven, he can speak eight languages)**
- **A auxiliary verb, an article, a pronoun , either subject or object. (example : it is easier to know)**
- **A comparative or superlative involved? (Example: she's taller than me)**

Previous Year Questions

Practice Set 1

Directions: In the following passage there are blanks, each of which has been numbered. These numbers are printed below the passage and against each, five words are suggested, one of which fits the blank appropriately. Find out the appropriate word in each case.

Actually every day we all are engaged in this business of reading people. We do it (__1__). We want to figure others out. So, we (__2__) make guesses about what others think, value, want and feel and we do so based on our (__3__) beliefs and understandings about human nature. We do so because if we can figure out (__4__) and intentions of others the possibility of them (__5__) or hurting us, (__6__) and this will help us to (__7__) a lot of unnecessary pain and trouble. We also make second guesses about what they will do in future, how they will (__8__) if we make this or that response. We do all this second guessing based upon our (__9__) of what we believe about the persons inner nature __10__) his or her roles and, manners. We mind read their fill (__11__) their motives. Also, every day we mis-guess and misread. Why? Because of the complexity, (__12__), and multidimensional functioning of people. After all how well do you read your own thoughts, aims, values, motives, beliefs etc.? How well do you know your own structuring process your own thinking and (__13__) styles?

Question 1

a) vehemently

b) practically

c) actually

d) incessantly

e) virtually

Question 2

a) ably

b) constantly

c) partly

d) largely

e) positively

Question 3

a) futuristic

b) proactive

c) reactive

d) decorative

e) assumptive

Question 4.

a) manifestations

b) expressions

c) motives

d) hopes

e) prospects

Question 5

a) tricking

b) blaming

c) furthering

d) alarming

e) criticizing

Question 6

a) lessens

b) happens

c) questions

d) deepens

e) laments

Question 7

a) approach

b) direct

c) avoid

d) implement

e) prepare

Question 8

a) solve

b) apply

c) plan

d) approach

e) react

Question 9

a) projection

b) exhibition

c) situation

d) perception

e) attribution

Question 10

a) organizing
b) underneath
c) appreciating
d) proposing
e) outside

Question 11

a) cunning
b) visible
c) deeper
d) obvious
e) proposed

Question 12

a) abnormality
b) angularity
c) focus
d) unpredictability
e) contribution

Question 13

a) proposing

b) developing

c) upbringing

d) lamenting

e) emoting

Correct Answer: 1 – d; 2 – b; 3 – e; 4 – c; 5 – b; 6 – a; 7 – c; 8 – e; 9 – d; 10 – a; 11 – c; 12 – d; 13 - e

Practice Set II

Directions: In the following passage there are blanks, each of which has been numbered. Against each number, five words are suggested, one of which fits the blank appropriately. Find out the appropriate word in each case.

After ten years of (__14__) inflation, prices have spiked 7.5% in the third week of July. This looks scary after all, Indians had got used to prices crawling up by 2% in the last two years, and a 10y ear average inflation rate of about 5% but you shouldn't worry. This burst of inflation is the result of three factors that have come together unexpectedly, are unlikely to (__15__) for long and are unlikely to (__16__) up together again. A (__17__) rise in global oil prices, a monsoon that arrived late and a spike in global metal prices. North Sea crude has crossed $42 per barrel, driven up by low petroleum (__18__) and soaring demand In the US as war production heats up. Oil markets are also spooked by the (__19__) of Russian oil supplies falling on the back of the Yukos Sibneft probe. There's little that the government can do to (__20__) users from soaring oil prices indeed, it shouldn't, if it wants to (__21__) efficiency. Higher transport costs have pushed up rates of vegetables and fruits farm produce could also get affected by rains that arrived too late for kharif sowing. China is (__22__) up steel and other metals from all over the world to (__23__) a construction boom ahead of the 2008 Olympics, making metal prices soar all over the world, and sparking inflation in India.

Question 14

a) mere

b) moderate

c) retarding

d) vehement

e) dull

Question 15

a) obstinate

b) constitute

c) persist

d) repeat

e) normalize

Question 16

a) go

b) scramble

c) mount

d) yield

e) crop

Question 17

a) sustained

b) suspicious

Question 18

a) lists

b) trades

Question 19

a) prospect

b) progress

c) horrific
d) erratic
e) favourable

c) services
d) inventories
e) details

c) view
d) extent
e) deposit

Question 20

a) support
b) ignore
c) propel
d) prolong
e) Insulate

Question 21

a) position
b) promote
c) process
d) pass
e) form

Question 22

a) hurrying
b) passing
c) pairing
d) gobbling
e) throwing

Question 23

a) keep
b) make
c) feed
d) grow
e) fight

Correct Answer: 14 – b; 15 – c; 16 – e; 17 – c; 18 – b; 19 – a; 20 – e; 21 – b; 22 – d; 23 - b

Practice Set III

Directions: **In the following passage there are blanks, each of which has been numbered. Against each number, five words are suggested, one of which fits the blank appropriately. Find out the appropriate word in each case.**

Though much theory has (__24__) little is really known about the power that lies at the (__25__) of scientific discoveries. It is true that great scientists and discoverers (__26__) discovery by employing all the (__27__) of personality and by fusing feelings, reasons and (__28__) But, what is the (__29__) synthesis that joins and (__30__) these complex parts into scientific invention? A famous scientist of yesteryears had developed one of the (__31__) and still generally (__32__) answers to this question. Imaginative (__33__) he concludes, is a complex process in which the conscious and the unconscious thinking processes jointly operate.

Question 24

a) gathered
b) amassed
c) collected
d) especially
e) accumulated

Question 25

a) climax
b) heart
c) foot
d) link
e) helm

Question 26

a) respect
b) treat
c) like
d) construct
e) appreciate

Question 27

a) enlightenment
b) control
c) exposure
d) variation
e) manifestations

Question 28

a) intuitions
b) invention
c) formation
d) outcomes
e) ambition

Question 29

a) scientific
b) miraculous
c) generally
d) reasoned
e) linking

Question 30

a) ravage
b) merges
c) arranges
d) deciphers
e) overstates

Question 31

a) most attractive
b) simplest
c) unswerving
d) best
e) original

Question 32

a) suggested
b) crucial
c) satisfactory
d) criticised
e) concourse

Question 33

a) prognosis
b) talent
c) content
d) discoveries
e) invention

Correct Answer: 24 – b; 25 – b; 26 – c; 27 – a; 28 – e; 29 – a; 30 – b; 31 – d; 32 – c; 33 - d

Practice Set IV

Directions: In the following passage there are blanks, each of which has been numbered. against each number, five words are suggested, one of which fits the blank appropriately. Find out the appropriate word in each case.

Most of us are (__34__) of open conflict and avoid it if we can. And there is a (__35__) to expressing and working through conflict. If the working through involves harsh words and name-calling people feel deeply hurt and relationships can be (__36__). Some- times permanently. Some group members may be afraid that if they really (__37__) their anger, they may go out of control and become violent, or they may do this. These fears can be very (__38__) and based on experience. So why take the risk? Why not avoid conflict at all costs? Conflict is rather like disease (__39__) is best, that means attuning to areas where (__40__) may occur before they become an issue. If you have, not (__41__) a conflict happening, your next choice is to treat it early, or hope that it goes away. If it goes away over time fine. If it (__42__), then you will still have to handle (treat) it and it is likely to be more (__43__).

Question 34

a) scared

b) careful

c) reckless

d) aware

e) worried

Question 35

a) challenge

b) measure

c) principle

d) chance

e) risk

Question 36

a) established

b) maligned

c) damaged

d) rebuilt

e) involved

Question 37

a) sublimate

b) express

c) minimize

d) regulate

e) control

Question 38

a) baseless

b) imaginary

c) exaggerative

d) real

e) national

Question 39

a) cure

b) diagnosis

c) prescription

d) prevention

e) medicine

Question 40

a) harmony

b) discomfiture

Question 41

a) expressed

b) ignored

Question 42

a) doesn’t

b) wont

c) disagreement
d) consensus
e) statement

c) induced
d) seen
e) perverted

c) don’t
d) not
e) hasn’t

Question 43

a) credible
b) serious
c) fraudulent
d) urgent
e) important

Correct Answer: 34 – a; 35 – e; - 36 – c; 37 – b; 38 – d; 39 – d; 40 – b; 41 – b; 42 – a; 43 - b

Direction:

The following questions, you have several passages where some of the words have been left out. Read the passages carefully and choose the correct answer to each blanks with its particular number, out of the five alternatives.

After ten years of ____(1)____ inflation, prices have hiked 7.5% in the third week of July. This looks scary—after all, Indians had got used to prices crawling up by 2% in the last two years, and a 10-year average inflation rate of about 5%—but you shouldn't worry. This burst of inflation is the result of three factors that have come together unexpectedly, are unlikely to ____(2)____ for long and are unlikely to ____(3)____ up together again: a____(n)____ ____(4)____ rise in global oil prices, a monsoon that arrived late and a spike in global metal prices. North Sea crude has crossed $42 per barrel, driven up by low petroleum ____(5)____ and soaring demand in the US as war production heats up. Oil markets are also spooked by the ____(6)____ of Russian oil supplies falling on the back of the YukosSibneft probe. There's little that the government can do to ____(7)____ users from soaring oil prices—indeed, it shouldn't, if it wants to ____(8)____ efficiency. Higher transport costs have pushed up rates of vegetables and fruits. Farm produce could also get affected by rains that arrived too late for kharif sowing. China is ____(9)____ up steel and other metals from all over the world to ____(10)____ a construction boom ahead of the 2008 Olympics, making metal prices soar all over the world, and sparking inflation in India.

1. Find the blank (1)?

a) mere

b) moderate

c) retarding

d) vehement

e) dull

Answer: (b)

2. Find the blank (2)?

a) obstinate

b) constitute

c) persist

d) repeat

e) normalize

Answer: (c)

3. Find the blank (3)?

a) go

b) scramble

c) mount

d) yield

e) crop

Answer: (e)

4. Find the blank (4)?

a) sustained

b) suspicious

c) horrific

d) erratic

e) favourable

Answer: (d)

5. Find the blank (5)?

a) lists

b) trades

c) services

d) inventories

e) details

Answer: (b)

6. Find the blank (6)?

a) prospect

b) progress

c) view

d) extent

e) deposit

Answer: (a)

7. Find the blank (7)?

a) support

b) ignore

c) propel

d) prolong

e) insulate

Answer: (e)

8. Find the blank (8)?

a) position

b) promote

c) process

d) pass

e) form

Answer: (b)

9. Find the blank (9)?

a) hurrying

b) passing

c) pairing

d) gobbling

e) throwing

Answer: (d)

10. Find the blank (10)?

a) keep

b) make

c) feed

d) grow

e) fight

Answer: (c)

Direction:

The following questions, you have several passages where some of the words have been left out. Read the passages carefully and choose the correct answer to each blanks with its particular number, out of the five alternatives.

The major central banks' ____(1)____negligent pursuit of positive but low inflation has become a dangerous ____(2)____delusion. It is dangerous because the policies needed to achieve the objective could have unwanted side effects; and it is a delusion because there is currently no good reason to be pursuing the objective in the first place. In the 1970s, when inflation in the advanced economies rose sharply, central banks rightly ____(3)____adhere it. The lesson central bankers took from that battle was that low infl is a necessary condition for sustained growth. But, subtly and over time, this lesson has ___(4)___morphed into a belief that low inflation is also a sufficient condition for sustained growth. That change may have been due to the benign economic conditions that accompanied the period of disinflation from the late 1980s to 2007, commonly ___(5)___suppress to as the "Great Moderation." For central bankers, it was comforting to believe that they had reduced inflation by controlling demand, and that their policies had many beneficial side effects for the economy. After all, this was the demand-oriented ___(6)___ refrain they had used to justify tight money to begin with. But then the world changed. From the late 1980s onward, low inflation was largely due to positive supply-side shocks – such as the Baby Boomer-fueled expansion of the labor force and the___(7)___hostility of many emerging countries into the global trading system. These forces boosted growth while lowering inflation. And monetary policy, far from restricting demand, was generally focused on preventing below-target inflation. As we now know, that led to a period of easy monetary conditions, which, together with financial deregulation and technological developments, ___(8)___sowed the seeds of the 2007 financial crisis and the ensuing recession. The fundamental analytical error then – as it still is today – was a failure to ___(9)___degrade between alternative sources of disinflation. The end of the Great ___(10)___indulgence should have disabused policymakers of their belief that low inflation guarantees future economic stability. If anything, the opposite has been true. Having doubled down on their inflation targets, central banks have had to rely on an unprecedented array of untested policy instruments to achieve their goals.

1. Which of the following words fits gap (1)?

a) breach

b) antagonization

c) vigilant

d) impulsive

e) No correction required.

Answer: (c) vigilant – keeping careful watch for possible danger or difficulties.

2. Which of the following words fits gap (2)?

a) discreet

b) surefire

c) withdrawal

d) humble

e) No correction required

Answer: (e) No correction required.

3. Which of the following words fits gap (3)?

a) attentive

b) intensity

c) conviction

d) resisted

e) No correction required.

Answer: (d) resisted – withstand the action or effect of.

4. Which of the following words fits gap (4)?

a) authoritativeness

b) outrageousness

c) credence

d) dogmatism

e) No correction required.

Answer: (e) No correction required.

5. Which of the following words fits gap (5)?

a) staunchness

b) referred

c) intemperance

d) assent

e) No correction required.

Answer: (b) referred – mention or allude to.

6. Which of the following words fits gap (6)?

a) narrative

b) steadiness

c) acquiesce

d) wildness

e) No correction required.

Answer: (a) narrative – a spoken or written account of connected events; a story.

7. Which of the following words fits gap (7)?

a) debase

b) alienation

c) integration

d) inhibit

e) No correction required.

8. Which of the following words fits gap (8)?

a) inevitability

b) knuckle

c) bidding

d) belittle

e) No correction required

9. Which of the following words fits gap (9)?

a) accede

b) disunity

c) forbear

d) distinguish

e) No correction required

Answer: (d) distinguish – recognize or treat (someone or something) as different.

10. Which of the following words fits gap (10)?

a) prevent

b) withholding

c) schism

d) Moderation

e) No correction required

Answer: (d) Moderation – the avoidance of excess or extremes, especially in one's behaviour or political opinions.

ONE WORD SUBSTITUTION

ONE WORD SUBSTITUTION

One word substitution is the use of one word in place of a wordy phrase in order to make the sentence structure clearer. The meaning, with the replacement of the phrase remains identical while the sentence becomes shorter.

Categories of One word Substitution

- Generic Terms
- Government/Systems
- Venue/Spots
- Group/Collection
- People/Person
- Murder/Death
- Profession/Research
- Sound

One Word Substitution for Generic Terms

An act of abdicating or renouncing the throne	Abdication
An annual calendar containing important dates and statistical information such as astronomical data and tide tables	Almanac
A cold-blooded vertebrate animal that is born in water and breathes with gills	Amphibian
A story, poem, or picture that can be interpreted to reveal a hidden meaning, typically a moral or political one	Allegory
A statement or proposition on which an abstractly defined structure is based	Axiom
A nation or person engaged in war or conflict, as recognized by international law	Belligerent
An examination of tissue removed from a living body to discover the presence, cause, or extent of a disease	Biopsy

The action or offence of speaking sacrilegiously about God or sacred things; profane talk	Blasphemy
The arrangement of events or dates in the order of their occurrence	Chronology
A vigorous campaign for political, social, or religious change	Crusade
Lasting for a very short time	Ephemeral
Spoken or done without preparation	Extempore
Release someone from a duty or obligation	Exonerate
Fond of company	Gregarious
Making marks that cannot be removed	Indelible
Incapable of making mistakes or being wrong	Infallible
Certain to happen	Inevitable
A sentimental longing or wistful affection for a period in the past	Nostalgia
A solution or remedy for all difficulties or diseases	Panacea
A doctrine which identifies God with the universe	Pantheism
Excessively concerned with minor details or rules	Pedantic
The practice of taking someone else's work or ideas and passing them off as one's own	Plagiarism
Safe to drink	Potable
The emblems or insignia of royalty	Regalia
Violation or misuse of what is regarded as sacred	Sacrilege
A position requiring little or no work but giving the holder status or financial benefit	Sinecure

A thing that is kept as a reminder of a person, place, or event	Souvenir
An imaginary ideal society free of poverty and suffering	Utopia
Denoting a sin that is not regarded as depriving the soul of divine grace	Venial
In exactly the same words as were used originally	Verbatim

One Word Substitution for Government/Systems

A state of disorder due to absence or non-recognition of authority or other controlling systems	Anarchy
A form of government in which power is held by the nobility	Aristocracy
A system of government by one person with absolute power	Autocracy
A self-governing country or region	Autonomy
A system of government in which most of the important decisions are taken by state officials rather than by elected representatives	Bureaucracy
A system of government by the whole population or all the eligible members of a state, typically through elected representatives	Democracy
A state, society, or group governed by old people	Gerontocracy
A state or country run by the worst, least qualified, or most unscrupulous citizens	Kakistocracy
Government by new or inexperienced hands	Neocracy
Government by the populace	Ochlocracy
A small group of people having control of a country or organization	Oligarchy
Government by the wealthy	Plutocracy
Government not connected with religious or spiritual matters	Secular

A form of government with a monarch at the head	Monarchy
A political system based on government of men by God	Thearchy

One Word Substitution for Venue OR Spot

A collection of historical documents or records providing information about a place, institution, or group of people	Archives
A large cage, building, or enclosure for keeping birds in	Aviary
A building where animals are butchered	Abattoir
A place where bees are kept; a collection of beehives	Apiary
A building containing tanks of live fish of different species	Aquarium
A place or scene of activity, debate, or conflict	Arena
A collection of weapons and military equipment	Arsenal
An institution for the care of people who are mentally ill	Asylum
A hole or tunnel dug by a small animal, especially a rabbit, as a dwelling	Burrow
A collection of items of the same type stored in a hidden or inaccessible place	Cache
A public room or building where gambling games are played	Casino
A large burial ground, especially one not in a churchyard	Cemetery
A room in a public building where outdoor clothes or luggage may be left	Cloakroom
A place where a dead person's body is cremated	Crematorium
a Christian community of nuns living together under monastic vows	Convent

Nursery where babies and young children are cared for during the working day	Creche
A stoppered glass container into which wine or spirit is decanted	Decanter
A large bedroom for a number of people in a school or institution	Dormitory
The nest of a squirrel, typically in the form of a mass of twigs in a tree	Drey
A room or building equipped for gymnastics, games, and other physical exercise	Gymnasium
A storehouse for threshed grain	Granary
A large building with an extensive floor area, typically for housing aircraft.	Hangar
A box or cage, typically with a wire mesh front, for keeping rabbits or other small domesticated animals	Hutch
A place in a large institution for the care of those who are ill	Infirmary
A small shelter for a dog	Kennel
A place where wild animal live	Lair
A place where coins, medals, or tokens are made	Mint
A collection of wild animals kept in captivity for exhibition	Menagerie
A building or buildings occupied by a community of monks living under religious vows	Monastery
A place where bodies are kept for identification	Morgue
A piece of enclosed land planted with fruit trees	Orchard
A large natural or artificial lake used as a source of water supply	Reservoir
A small kitchen or room at the back of a house used for washing dishes and another dirty household work	Scullery

A close-fitting cover for the blade of a knife or sword	Sheath
A room or building for sick children in a boarding school	Sanatorium
A place where animal hides are tanned	Tannery
A large, tall cupboard in which clothes may be hung or stored	Wardrobe

One Word Substitution for Group/Collection

A group of guns or missile launchers operated together at one place	Battery
A large bundle bound for storage or transport	Bale
A large gathering of people of a particular type	Bevy
An arrangement of flowers that is usually given as a present	Bouquet
A family of young animals	Brood
A group of things that have been hidden in a secret place	Cache
A group of people, typically with vehicles or animals travelling together	Caravan
A closed political meeting	Caucus
An exclusive circle of people with a common purpose	Clique
A group of followers hired to applaud at a performance	Claque
A series of stars	Constellation
A funeral procession	Cortege
A group of worshippers	Congregation
A herd or flock of animals being driven in a body	Drove

A small fleet of ships or boats	Flotilla
A small growth of trees without underbrush	Grove
A community of people smaller than a village	Hamlet
A group of cattle or sheep or other domestic mammals	Herd
A large group of people	Horde
A temporary police force	Posse
A large number of fish swimming together	Shoal
A strong and fast-moving stream of water or other liquid	Torrent

One Word Substitution List for Person or People

One who is not sure about God's existence	Agnostic
A person who deliberately sets fire to a building	Arsonist
One who does a thing for pleasure and not as a profession	Amateur
One who can use either hand with ease	Ambidextrous
One who makes an official examination of accounts	Auditor
A person who believes in or tries to bring about a state of lawlessness	Anarchist
A person who has changed his faith	Apostate
One who does not believe in the existence of God	Atheist
A person appointed by two parties to solve a dispute	Arbitrator
One who leads an austere life	Ascetic

One who does a thing for pleasure and not as a profession	Amateur
One who can either hand with ease	Ambidextrous
An unconventional style of living	Bohemian
One who is bad in spellings	Cacographer
One who feeds on human flesh	Cannibal
A person who is blindly devoted to an idea/ A person displaying aggressive or exaggerated patriotism	Chauvinist
A critical judge of any art and craft	Connoisseur
Persons living at the same time	Contemporaries
One who is recovering health after illness	Convalescent
A girl/woman who flirts with man	Coquette
A person who regards the whole world as his country	Cosmopolitan
One who is a centre of attraction	Cynosure
One who sneers at the beliefs of others	Cynic
A leader or orator who espoused the cause of the common people	Demagogue
A person having a sophisticated charm	Debonair
A leader who sways his followers by his oratory	Demagogue
A dabbler (not serious) in art, science and literature	Dilettante
One who is for pleasure of eating and drinking	Epicure
One who often talks of his achievements	Egotist
Someone who leaves one country to settle in another	Emigrant

A man who is womanish in his habits	Effeminate
One hard to please (very selective in his habits)	Fastidious
One who runs away from justice	Fugitive
One who is filled with excessive enthusiasm in religious matters	Fanatic
One who believes in fate	Fatalist
A lover of good food	Gourmand
Conferred as an honour	Honorary
A person who acts against religion	Heretic
A person of intellectual or erudite tastes	Highbrow
A patient with imaginary symptoms and ailments	Hypochondriac
A person who is controlled by wife	Henpeck
One who shows sustained enthusiastic action with unflagging vitality	Indefatigable
Someone who attacks cherished ideas or traditional institutions	Iconoclast
One who does not express himself freely	Introvert
Who behaves without moral principles	Immoral
A person who is incapable of being tampered with	Impregnable
One who is unable to pay his debts	Insolvent
A person who is mentally ill	Lunatic
A person who dislikes humankind and avoids human society	Misanthrope
A person who primarily concerned with making money at the expense of ethics	Mercenary

Someone in love with himself	Narcissist
One who collect coins as hobby	Numismatist
A person who likes or admires women	Philogynist
A lover of mankind	Philanthropist
A person who speaks more than one language	Polyglot
One who lives in solitude	Recluse
Someone who walks in sleep	Somnambulist
A person who is indifferent to the pains and pleasures of life	Stoic
A scolding nagging bad-tempered woman	Termagant
A person who shows a great or excessive fondness for one's wife	Uxorious
One who possesses outstanding technical ability in a particular art or field	Virtuoso

One Word Substitution for Death/Murder

A solemn procession, especially for a funeral	Cortege
A poem of serious reflection, typically a lament for the dead	Elegy
A phrase or form of words written in memory of a person who has died	Epitaph
Killing of one's son or daughter	Filicide
Destruction or abortion of a fetus	Foeticide
Killing of one's brother or sister	Fratricide
Killing of a large group of people	Genocide

Killing of one person by another	Homicide
Killing of infants	Infanticide
Burial of a corpse in a grave or tomb	Interment
Killing of one's mother	Matricide
A room or building in which dead bodies are kept	Mortuary
A news article that reports the recent death of a person	Obituary
Killing of a parent or other near relative	Parricide
Killing of one's father	Patricide
An examination of a dead body to determine the cause of death	Postmortem
Action of killing a king	Regicide
Killing of one's sister	Sororicide
Act of intentionally causing one's own death	Suicide
Killing of one's wife	Uxoricide

List of One Word Substitutes for Profession/Research

The medieval forerunner of chemistry	Alchemy
A person who presents a radio/television programme	Anchor
One who studies the evolution of mankind	Anthropologist
A person who is trained to travel in a spacecraft	Astronaut
The scientific study of the physiology, structure, genetics, ecology, distribution, classification, and economic importance of plants	Botany

A person who draws or produces maps	Cartographer
A person who writes beautiful writing	Calligrapher
A person who composes the sequence of steps and moves for a performance of dance	Choreographer
A person employed to drive a private or hired car	Chauffeur
A person who introduces the performers or contestants in a variety show	Compere
A keeper or custodian of a museum or other collection	Curator
The branch of biology concerned with cyclical physiological phenomena	Chronobiology
A secret or disguised way of writing	Cypher
The study of statistics	Demography
The use of the fingers and hands to communicate and convey ideas	Dactylology
A person who sells and arranges cut flowers	Florist
A line of descent traced continuously from an ancestor	Genealogy
The therapeutic use of sunlight	Heliotherapy
The art or practice of garden cultivation and management	Horticulture
One who supervises in the examination hall	Invigilator
The theory or philosophy of law	Jurisprudence
A person who compiles dictionaries	Lexicographer
The scientific study of the structure and diseases of teeth	Odontology
One who presents a radio programme	Radio Jockey
The art of effective or persuasive speaking or writing	Rhetoric

The branch of science concerned with the origin, structure, and composition of rocks	Petrology
One who study the elections and trends in voting	Psephologist
An artist who makes sculptures.	Sculptor
The scientific study of the behaviour, structure, physiology, classification, and distribution of animals	Zoology

One Word Substitution for Sound

The branch of physics concerned with the properties of sound	Acoustics
The sound of Alligators	Bellow
The sound of Deers	Bell
The sound of Crows	Caw
The sound of Geese	Cackle
The sound of Hens	Cluck
The sound of Dolphins	Click
The sound of Frogs	Croak
The sound of Crickets	Creak
The sound of Monkeys	Gibber
The sound of Camels	Grunt
The sound of Owls	Hoot
The sound of Penguins	Honk
The sound of Cattle	Moo

1. Medicine given to counteract poison

(A) Antiseptic

(B) Antidote

(C) Antibiotic

(D) Anti fungal

(E) None of these

Answer: (B) Antidote

2. Person who files a suit

(A) Accuse

(B) Plaintiff

(C) Suitor

(D) Charger

(E) Adapter
Answer: (B) Plaintiff

3. A person who abstains completely from alcoholic drinks
(A) Incriminatory

(B) Subjunctive

(C) Derelict

(D) Teetotaller

(E) None of these

Answer: (D) Teetotaller

4. The practice of having many wives

(A) Polyandry

(B) Polygamy

(C) Calligraphy

(D) Bigamy
(E) None of these

Answer: (B) Polygamy

5. One who is not likely to be easily pleased

(A) Fastidious

(B) Fatalist

(C) Communist

(D) Infallible

(E) None of these

Answer: (A) Fastidious

6. One who hates marriage

(A) Misanthrope

(B) Polygamist

(C) Misogynist

(D) Misogamist

(E) None of these

Answer: (D) Misogamist

7. One who specialises in the mathematics of insurance

(A) A statistician

(B) An actuary

(C) An agent

(D) An insurer

(E) None of these
Answer: (B) An actuary

8. One who is always doubting

(A) Positivist

(B) Rationalist

(C) Deist

(D) Sceptic

(E) None of these

Answer: (D) Sceptic

9. A strong dislike
(A) Reciprocity

(B) Entreaty

(C) Malice

(D) Animosity

(E) None of these
Answer: (D) Animosity

10. Violation of the sanctity of the Church
(A) Infringement

(B) Irreverence

(C) Transgression

(D) Sacrilege

(E) None of these

Answer: (D) Sacrilege

11. The depository where state records and documents are preserved.
(A) Archive

(B) Emporium

(C) Library

(D) Museum

(E) None of these

Answer: (A) Archive

12. A place where birds are kept

(A) Apiary

(B) Aquarium

(C) House

(D) Aviary

(E) None of these

Answer: (A) Apiary

13. One who is incapable of making errors

(A) Inexplicable

(B) Impervious

(C) Infallible

(D) Incorrigible

(E) None of htese

Answer: (C) Infallible

14. An assembly of worshipers is called

(A) Congregation

(B) Conflagration

(C) Configuration

(D) Confrontation

(E) None of these

Answer: (A) Congregation

15. A person who lives by himself

(A) Prophet

(B) Extrovert

(C) Recluse

(D) Monk

Answer: (C) Recluse

16. The act of producing beautiful handwriting using a brush or a special pen

(A) Graphics

(B) Stencilling

(C) Calligraphy

(D) Hieroglyphics

(E) None of these

Answer: (C) Calligraphy

17. A person who is well known in an unfavourable way

(A) Obscure

(B) Conspicuous

(C) Notorious

(D) Ethical

(E) None of these

Answer: (C) Notorious

18. One who performs daring gymnastic feats

(A) Conjurer

(B) Acrobat

(C) Juggler

(D) Athlete

(E) None of these

Answer: (B) Acrobat

19. Person who wastes his money on luxury

(A) Extempore

(B) Thrifty

(C) Promiscuous

(D) Extravagant

(E) None of these

Answer: (D) Extravagant

20. Rebellion against lawful authority

(A) Dissidence

(B) Mutiny

(C) Revolution

(D) Coup

(E) None of these

Answer: (B) Mutiny

ANTONYMS AND SYNONYMS

Synonyms and Antonyms

- Antonyms and Synonyms are asked in the English section of various government exams.
- A synonym is a word/phrase, the meaning of which is the same or nearly the same as another word or phrase. Words that are synonyms are described as synonymous.
- An antonym is a word/phrase that means the opposite of another word or phrase.
- The best way to prepare Antonyms and Synonyms for exams is to daily learn words and their meaning, their synonyms, and antonyms.
- It will help the students broaden their vocabulary and solve the questions.

Words	Synonyms	Antonyms
Abate	Moderate, decrease	Aggravate
Adhere	Comply, observe	Condemn, disjoin
Abolish	Abrogate, annul	Setup, establish
Acumen	Awareness, brilliance	Stupidity, ignorance
Abash	Disconcert, rattle	Uphold, Discompose
Absolve	Pardon, forgive	Compel, Accuse
Abjure	Forsake, renounce	Approve, Sanction
Abject	Despicable, servile	Commendable, Praiseworthy
Abound	Flourish, proliferate	Deficient, Destitute
Abortive	Vain, unproductive	Productive
Acrimony	Harshness, bitterness	Courtesy, Benevolence
Accord	Agreement, harmony	Discord

Adjunct	Joined, Added	Separated, Subtracted
Adversity	Misfortune, calamity	Prosperity, Fortune
Adherent	Follower, disciple	Rival, Adversary
Adamant	Stubborn, inflexible	Flexible, Soft
Admonish	Counsel, reprove	Approve, Applaud
Allay	Pacify, soothe	Aggravate, Excite
Alien	Foreigner, outsider	Native, Resident
Ascend	Climb Escalate	Descend, Decline
Alleviate	Abate, relieve	Aggravate, Enhance
Allure	Entice, fascinate	Repulse, Repel
Arraign	Incriminate, indict	Exculpate, Pardon
Amplify	Augment, deepen	Lessen, Contract
Axiom	Adage, truism	Absurdity, Blunder
Audacity	Boldness, Courage	Mildness, Cowardice
Authentic	Accurate, credible	Fictitious, unreal
Awkward	Rude, blundering	Adroit, clever
Barbarous	Frustrate, perplex	Civilized
Bleak	Grim, Austere	Bright, Pleasant
Bewitching	Alluring, charming	Repulsive, Repugnant

Baroque	Florid, gilt	Plain, unadorned
Brittle	Breakable, crisp	Tough, Enduring
Barrier	Barricade, Obstacle	Link, Assistance
Baffle	Astound, Faze	Facilitate, Clarify
Bustle	Commotion, Tumult	Slowness, Quiet
Barren	Desolate, Sterile	Damp, Fertile
Bawdy	Erotic, Coarse	Decent, Moral
Bind	Predicament	Release
Batty	Insane, silly	Sane
Benevolent	Benign, Generous	Malevolent, Miserly
Befogged	Becloud, Dim	Clear headed, Uncloud
Base	Vulgar, Coarse	Summit, Noble
Benign	Favorable, friendly	Malignant, Cruel
Busy	Active, Engaged	Idle, Lazy
Bleak	Austere, Blank	Bright, Cheerful
Bold	Adventurous	Timid
Boisterous	Clamorous, rowdy	Placid, Calm
Blunt	Dull, Insensitive	Keen, Sharp
Callous	obdurate, unfeeling	Compassionate, Tender

Capable	competent, able	Incompetent, Inept
Calamity	adversity, misfortune	Fortune
Calculating	Canny, Devious	Artless, honest
Calumny	defamation, aspersion	Commendation, Praise
Captivity	imprisonment, confinement	Freedom, Liberty
Captivate	Charm, fascinate	Disillusion offend
Chaste	virtuous, pure	Sullied, Lustful
Cease	terminate, desist	Begin, Originate
Compassion	kindness, sympathy	Cruelty, Barbarity
Chastise	punish, admonish	Cheer, encourage
Concede	yield, permit	Deny, reject
Comprise	include, contain	Reject, lack
Consent	agree, permit	Object Disagree
Concur	approve, agree	Differ, disagree
Consolidate	solidify, strengthen	Separate, Weaken
Consequence	effect, outcome	Origin, Start
Contempt	scorn, disregard	Regard, Praise
Conspicuous	prominent, obvious	Concealed, hidden
Contrary	dissimilar, conflicting	Similar, Alike

Contradict	deny, oppose	Approve, Confirm
Callous	Insensitive, indurated	Kind, merciful
Calm	Harmonious, unruffled	Stormy, turbulent
Candid	Blunt, bluff	Evasive
Camouflage	Cloak, disguise	Reveal
Carnal	Earthly, fleshly	Spiritual
Captivate	Beguile, bewitch	Repel
Celebrated	Acclaimed, lionized	Unknown, Inglorious
Catholic	Generic, liberal	Narrow- minded
Censure	Rebuke, reprimand	Praise, Acceptance
Cement	Plaster, mortar	Disintegrate
Clandestine	Covert, furtive	Open, Legal
Cheap	Competitive, Inexpensive	Dear, unreasonable
Coarse	Bawdy, Boorish	Fine, Chaste
Classic	Simple, Typical	Romantic, Unusual
Compact	Bunched, thick	Loose, Diffuse
Comic	Clown, Jester	Tragic, tragedian
Conceit	Egotism, Immodesty	Modesty
Compress	Abbreviate, Shrink	Amplify, Expand

Condemn	Castigate, Chide	Approve, Praise
Concord	Agreement, accord	Discord
Consolidate	Centralize, Fortify	Weaken
Confident	Bold, Undaunted	Diffident, cowardly
Creation	Formation, foundation	Destruction
Courtesy	Generosity, Reverence	Disdain, Rudeness
Cunning	Acute, Smart	Naive, Coarse
Decipher	interpret, reveal	Misinterpret, distort
Decay	Collapse, decompose	Flourish, Progress
Deceit	deception, artifice	Veracity, Sincerity
Defray	spend, pay	Disclaim, Repudiate
Defile	contaminate, pollute	Purify, sanctity
Demolish	Ruin, devastate	Repair, construct
Deliberate	cautious, intentional	Rash, Sudden
Deride	mock, taunt	Inspire, Encourage
Deprive	despoil, divest	Restore, Renew
Dissuade	Remonstrate, Counsel	Insite, Persuade
Disdain	detest, despise	Approve, praise
Dense	Opaque, piled	Sparse, brainy

Denounce	Blame, boycott	Defend
Despair	Depression, misery	Contentment, Hope
Derogatory	Sarcastic, critical	Laudatory, appreciative
Docile	Pliable, pliant	Headstrong, obstinate
Destructive	Catastrophic, pernicious	Creative, Constructive
Dwarf	Diminutive, Petite	Huge, Giant
Eclipse	Diminution, Dimming	Shine, eclipse
Eager	Keen, acquisitive	Indifferent, apathetic
Ecstasy	delight, exultation	Despair, Calamity
Eccentric	strange, abnormal	Natural, Conventional
Encumbrance	hindrance, obstacle	Incentive, stimulant
Efface	destroy, obliterate	Retain, Maintain
Eloquence	expression, fluency	Halting, Stammering
Enormous	colossal, mammoth	Diminutive, negligible
Endeavour	undertake, aspire	Cease, quit
Equivocal	uncertain, hazy	Obvious, lucid
Epitome	precise, example	Increment, expansion
Eradicate	destroy, exterminate	Secure, plant
Fallacy	delusion, mistake	Veracity, Truth

Fabricate	construct, produce	Destroy, Dismantle
Fanatical	narrow-minded, biased	Liberal, Tolerant
Falter	stumble, demur	Persist, Endure
Ferocious	cruel, fierce	Gentle, Sympathetic
Feeble	weak, frail	Strong, Robust
Fluctuate	deflect, vacillate	Stabilize, resolve
Feud	strife, quarrel	Harmony, fraternity
Fragile	weak, infirm	Enduring, Tough
Forsake	desert, renounce	Hold, maintain
Frivolous	petty, worthless	Solemn, significant
Frantic	violent, agitated	Subdued, gentle
Frugality	economy, providence	Lavishness, extravagance
Gloom	obscurity, darkness	Delight, mirth
Gather	Converge, huddle	Disperse, Dissemble
Gorgeous	magnificent, dazzling	Dull, unpretentious
Glut	stuff, satiate	Starve, abstain
Grisly	disgusting, atrocious	Pleasing, attractive
Gracious	courteous, beneficent	Rude, Unforgiving
Guile	cunning, deceit	Honesty, frankness

Grudge	hatred, aversion	Benevolence, Affection
Genuine	Absolute, Factual	Spurious
Generosity	Altruism, bounty	Stinginess, greed
Glory	Dignity, renown	Shame, Disgrace
Gloomy	Bleak, cloudy	Gay, Bright
Harass	irritate, molest	Assist, comfort
Hamper	retard, prevent	Promote, facilitate
Hazard	Peril, danger	Conviction, security
Hapless	unfortunate, ill-fated	Fortunate, Lucky
Haughty	arrogant, pompous	Humble, Submissive
Hideous	frightful, shocking	Attractive, alluring
Heretic	non-conformist, secularist	Conformable, religious
Harmony	Conformity, Amicability	Discord, discord
Hamstrung	Cripple Debilitate	Strengthen, Encourage
Honor	Adoration, Reverence	Denunciation, Shame
Hasty	Abrupt, Impetuous	Leisurely, Cautious
Humility	Resignation, Fawning	Boldness, Pride
Humble	Meek, Timid	Proud, Assertive
Impenitent	Uncontrite, Obdurate	Repentant

Hypocrisy	Deception, Pharisaism	Sincerity, frankness
Indifferent	Equitable, Haughty	Partial, Biased
Impulsive	Flaky, Impetuous	Cautious, Deliberate
Infernal	Damned, Accursed	Heavenly,
Indigent	Destitute, Impoverished	Rich, Affluent
Interesting	Enchanting, Riveting	Dull, Uninteresting
Insipid	Tedious, Prosaic	Pleasing, appetizing
Immense	huge, enormous	Puny, Insignificant
Immaculate	unsullied, spotless	Defiled, Tarnished
Imminent	impending, brewing	Distant, Receding
Immerse	submerge, involve	Emerge, uncover
Impair	diminish, deteriorate	Restore, Revive
Immunity	prerogative, privilege	Blame, Censure
Impediment	hurdle, obstruction	Assistant, Concurrence
Impartial	just, unbiased	Prejudiced, Biased
Impute	attribute, ascribe	Exculpate, support
Impious	irreligious, unholy	Pious, Devout
Incompetent	inefficient, unskilled	Dexterous, Skilled
Inclination	disposition, affection	Indifference, Disinclination

Inevitable	unavoidable, ascertained	Unlikely, Doubtful
Incongruous	inappropriate, absurd	Compatible, harmonious
Ingenuous	undisguised, naive	Wily, Craftly
Infringe	violate, encroach	Comply, Concur
Insipid	tasteless, vapid	Delicious, luscious
Insinuate	allude, hint	Conceal, Camouflage
Instill	inculcate, inject	Eradicate, extract
Insolvent	indigent, destitute	Wealthy, solvent
Intrigue	scheme, conspiracy	Candor, Sincerity
Intricate	tangled, complicated	Regulated, Orderly
Invective	accusation, censure	Approval, acclamation
Intrinsic	genuine, fundamental	Extraneous, incidental
Immaculate	Exquisite, Impeccable	Defiled, Tarnished
Invincible	unconquerable, impregnable	Effeminate, languid
Irrepressible	irresistible, unconfined	Composed, hesitant
Jejune	dull, boring	Interesting, exciting
Jaded	tired, exhausted	Renewed, recreated
Jubilant	rejoicing, triumphant	Melancholy, depressing
Jovial	frolicsome, cheerful	Solemn, morose

Just	honest, impartial	Unequal, unfair
Judicious	thoughtful, prudent	Irrational, foolish
Juvenile	young, tender	Dotage, antiquated
Justify	defend, exculpate	Impute, arraign
Knave	dishonest, scoundrel	Paragon, innocent
Knotty	complicated difficult	Simple, manageable
Kindred	relation, species	Unrelated, dissimilar
Keen	sharp, poignant	Vapid, insipid
Knell	death knell, last blow	Reconstruction, rediscovery
Lax	slack, careless	Firm, reliable
Lavish	abundant, excessive	Scarce, deficient
Liable	accountable, bound	Unaccountable, apt to
Lenient	compassionate, merciful	Cruel, severe
Lucid	sound, rational	Obscure, hidden
Lure	attract, entice	Repel, dissuade
Linger	loiter, prolong	Hasten, quicken
Liberal	magnanimous, generous	Stingy, malicious
Lunacy	delusion, insanity	Normalcy, sanity
Luxuriant	profuse, abundant	Scanty, meagre

Luscious	palatable, delicious	Unsavory, tart
Languid	Sluggish, apathetic	Energetic, spirited
Mandatory	Imperative, requisite	Optional
Malice	Vengefulness, grudge	Goodwill, Kindness
Merit	Stature, Asset	Demerit, dishonor
Masculine	Gallant, strapping	Feminine, meek
Mitigate	alleviate, relieve	Augment enhance
Miraculous	marvelous, extraordinary	Ordinary, trivial
Molest	harass, tease	Console, soothe
Modest	humble, courteous	Arrogant, pompous
Momentous	notable, eventful	Trivial, insignificant
Mollify	appease, assuage	Irritate, infuriate
Morbid	Nasty, Macabre	Healthy, Cheerful
Monotonous	irksome, tedious	Varied, pleasant
Murky	dusky, dreary	Bright, shining
Munificent	liberal, hospitable	Frugal, penurious
Mutual	joint, identical	Separate, distinct
Mutinous	recalcitrant, insurgent	Submissive, faithful
Nimble	prompt, brisk	Sluggish, languid

Niggardly	miser, covetous	Generous, profuse
Noxious	baneful, injurious	Healing, profitable
Notion	Conceit, Apprehension	Reality, Concrete
Novice	tyro, beginner	Veteran, ingenious
Nonchalant	indifferent, negligent	Attentive, considerate
Nullify	cancel, annual	Confirm, Uphold
Numerous	profuse, various	Scarce, deficient
Obliging	Complaisant, Willing	Mulish, Obstinate
Obstruct	impede, prevent	Hasten, encourage
Obstinate	Stubborn, Adamant	Pliable, flexible
Obscure	Arcane, Vague	Prominent
Obvious	Evident, apparent	Obscure, ambiguous
Obtain	Access, Inherit	Forfeit
Offensive	Abhorrent, obnoxious	Engaging, fascinating
Odious	Malevolent, obnoxious	Engaging, fascinating
Offspring	descendant, sibling	Ancestor, forefather
Occult	latent, ambiguous	Intelligible, transparent
Opaque	obscure, shady	Transparent, bright
Ominous	Menacing, Foreboding	Auspicious

Oracular	cryptic, vague	Lucid, distinct
Optimist	Idealist	Pessimist
Ornamental	decorative, adorned	Unseemly, plain
Ordain	Order, impose	Revoke abolish
Outrage	offence, maltreatment	Praise, favour
Outbreak	eruption, insurrection	Compliance, subjection
Persuade	Cajole, Impress	Dissuade, halt
Pacify	Appease, Chasten	Irritate, worsen
Propagate	Inseminate, fecundate	Suppress, deplete
Perturbed	Flustered, anxious	Calm
Prompt	Precise, Punctual	Slow, Negligent
Progress	Pace, Betterment	Retrogress, worsening
Pamper	Flatter, indulge	Deny, disparage
Prudence	Vigilance, Discretion	Indiscretion
Peerless	matchless, unrivalled	Mediocre, commonplace
Paramount	foremost, eminent	Trivial, inferior
Pertness	flippancy, impudence	Modesty, diffidence
Peevish	perverse, sullen	Suave, amiable
Placid	tranquil, calm	Turbulent, hostile

Perverse	petulant, obstinate	Complacent, docile
Precarious	doubtful, insecure	Assured
Pompous	haughty, arrogant	Unpretentious, humble
Predicament	plight, dilemma	Resolution, confidence
Quaint	Queer, strange	Familiar, usual
Quack	Impostor, deceiver	Upright, unfeigned
Quell	subdue, reduce	Exacerbate, agitate
Quarantine	seclude, screen	Befriend, socialize
Quibble	equivocate, prevaricate	Unfeigned, plain
Rapidity	Quickness, Velocity	Inertia, lanquidity
Raid	Incursion, Foray	Retreat, release
Rebellious	Restless, attacking	Submissive, Compliant
Reason	Acumen, Bounds	Folly, Speculation
Reluctant	Cautious, Averse	anxious, Eager
Rectify	Amend, Remedy	Falsify, Worsen
Ravage	Destroy, ruin	Reconstruct, renovate
Remnant	Residue, piece	Entire, whole
Ratify	consent, approve	Deny, dissent
Restrain	Detain, Confine	Incite

Redeem	Recover, liberate	Conserve lose
Remorse	Regret, penitence	Ruthlessness, obduracy
Remonstrate	Censure, protest	Agree, loud
Resentment	Displeasure, wrath	Content, Cheer
Rescind	Annul, abrogate	Delegate, permit
Reverence	Respect, esteem	Disrespect, affront
Retract	Recant, withdraw	Confirm, assert
Rustic	Rural, uncivilized	Cultured, Refined
Rout	Vanquish, overthrow	Succumb, withdraw
Ruthless	Remorseless, inhumane	Compassionate, lenient
Savage	Wild, untamed	Polished, Civilized
Sacred	Cherish, Divine	Ungodly, Profane
Steep	Course, lofty	Flat, gradual
Startled	Frightened, Shocked	Waveringly
Sublime	Magnificent, eminent	Ridiculous
Stranger	Immigrant, guest	Acquaintance, national
Sympathy	Tenderness, harmony	Antipathy, Discord
Succinct	Concise, Terse	Lengthy, polite
Sarcastic	Ironical, derisive	Courteous, gracious

System	Scheme, Entity	Chaos, Disorder
Shrewd	Cunning, craftly	Simple, imbecile
Saucy	Impudent, insolent	Modest, humble
Servile	Slavish, Docile	Aggressive, Dominant
Scanty	scarce, insufficient	Lavish, multitude
Slander	defame, malign	Applaud, approve
Shabby	miserable, impoverished	Prosperous, thriving
Solicit	entreat, implore	Protest oppose
Sneer	mock, scorn	Flatter, praise
Stain	blemish, tarnish	Honor, purify
Subterfuge	Deceit, Stratagem	Frankness, Openness
Sporadic	intermittent, scattered	Incessant, frequent
Spurious	Fake, Counterfeit	Genuine, Authentic
Squalid	dirty, filthy	Tidy, Attractive
Spry	Nimble, Brisk	Lethargic, Sluggish
Sterile	Barren, Impotent	Profitable, Potent
Successful	Propitious, Felicitous	Destitute, Untoward
Subsequent	consequent, following	Preceding, previous
Stupor	lethargy, unconsciousness	Sensibility, Consciousness

Subvert	Demolish, sabotage	Generate, organize
Substantial	Considerable, solid	Tenuous, fragile
Sycophant	Parasite, flatterer	Devoted, loyal
Superficial	Partial, shallow	Profound, discerning
Taciturn	Reserved, silent	Talkative, extrovert
Taboo	Prohibit, ban	Permit, consent
Temperate	Cool, moderate	Boisterous, violent
Tedious	Wearisome. Irksome	Exhilarating, lively
Tenacious	Stubborn, Dodge	Docile, non- resinous
Tenement	Apartment, Digs	Breakeven, dislodge
Timid	Diffident, coward	Bold, intrepid
Throng	Assembly, crowd	Dispersion, sparsity
Transient	Temporal, transitory	Lasting, enduring
Tranquil	Peaceful, composed	Violent, furious
Treacherous	Dishonest, duplicitous	Forthright, reliable
Trenchant	Assertive, forceful	Feeble, ambiguous
Tumultuous	Violent, riotous	Peaceful, harmonious
Trivial	Trifling, insignificant	Significant, veteran
Tame	Compliant, Subdued	Wild, untamed

Tyro	Beginner, riotous	Proficient, veteran
Thick	Chunky, massive	Thin, attenuated
Terse	Incisive, Compact	Diffuse, Gentle
Tranquil	Amicable, Calm	Agitated, Fierce
Thrifty	Frugal, prudent	Extravagant
Tremble	Vibrate	Steady
Transparent	Diaphanous	Opaque
Utterly	Completely, entirely	Deficiently, incomplete
Uncouth	Awkward, ungraceful	Elegant, Compensate
Uncouth	Boorish, Clownish	Elegant, Compensate
Umbrage	Chagrin, offense	Sympathy, goodwill
Urge	Incite, Implore	Abhorrence, Abomination
Urchin	Foundling, Orphan	Creep, Knave
Vagrant	Wander, roaming	Steady, settled
Vain	Arrogant, egoistic	Modest
Vanity	Conceit, pretension	Modesty, Humility
Valor	Bravery, prowess	Fear, cowardice
Venom	Poison, malevolence	Antidote, Benevolent
Venerable	Esteemed, honored	Unworthy, immature

Vicious	Corrupt, obnoxious	Noble, Virtuous
Veteran	Ingenious, experienced	Novice, tyro
Vivacious	Spirited, Energetic	Dispirited, Unattractive
Vigilant	Cautious, alert	Careless, negligent
Vouch	Confirm, consent	Repudiate, prohibit
Vilify	Malign, Slur, Defame	Cherish, Commend
Vivid	Eloquent, lucid	Dull, Dim
Virtue	Ethic, morality	Vice, dishonesty
Wan	Pale, faded	Bright, healthy
Waive	Relinquish, remove	Impose, Clamp
Wary	cautious, circumspect	Heedless, negligent
Wane	Decline, Dwindle	Ameliorate, Rise
Wicked	vicious, immoral	Virtuous, Noble
Wed	marry, combine	Divorce, Separate
Wile	Trickery, Artifice	Naivety, honor
Wield	Exert, employ	Forgo, avoid
Wilt	wither, perish	Revive, bloom
Winsome	Beautiful, Comely	Alluring, Rapturous
Yield	surrender abdicate	Resist, protest

Yell	shout, shriek	Whisper muted
Yoke	connect, harness	Liberate, Release
Yearn	languish, crave	Content, satisfy
Zenith	summit, apex	Nadir, base
Zeal	eagerness, fervor	Apathy, lethargy
Zig -zag	oblique, wayward	Straight, unbent
Zest	delight, enthusiasm	Disgust, passive

1. She **detests** government jobs.

(A) Adores

(B) Approves of

(C) Is fond of

(D) Is interested in

(E) None of these

Ans: A

2. Her character is very **mild**.

(A) Rude

(B) Bad

(C) Gentle

(D) Angry

(E) None of these

Ans: C

3. His brother was a **brave** soldier.

(A) Noble

(B) Clever

(C) Coward

(D) Courageous

(E) None of these

Ans: C

4. The new officer is a **brash** young man.

(A) Arrogant

(B) Handsome

(C) Kind

(D) Polite

(E) None of these

Ans: D

5. Many snakes are **innocuous**.

(A) Harmful

(B) Deadly

(C) Ferocious

(D) Poisonous

(E) None of these

Ans: A

6. He has a **delicate** constitution.

(A) Rugged

(B) Strong

(C) Ungainly

(D) Fit

(E) None of these

Ans: B

7. She is **slender** in figure.

(A) Slim

(B) Shout

(C) Strong

(D) Well-built

(E) None of these

Ans: B

8. It was a **voluntary** gesture.

(A) Valuable

(B) Deliberate

(C) Violent

(D) Compulsory

(E) None of these

Ans: D

9. Suganya is a **smart** girl.

(A) Active

(B) Lazy

(C) Indecent

(D) Casual

(E) None of these

Ans: B

10. Life in the villages is very **dull**.

(A) Pleasant

(B) Bluffing

(C) Wasteful

(D) Serious

(E) None of these

Ans: A

11. Find the synonym of the following word **Frantically**

A Satisfactory

B Amok

C Calmly

D Meak

Answer : B

12. Find the synonym of the following word **Narcissist**

A humble

B altruistic

C braggart

D shy

E None of these

Answer : C

13. One who treats hearing **difficulties**:

A a dermatologist

B an audiologist

C an internist

D an ophthalmologist

E None of these

Answer : B

14. Find the synonym of the following word **Faux pas**
A correction

B right

C blooper

D fix

E None of these

Answer : C

15. Find the synonym of the following word **Component**

A secondary

B inherent

C additional

D extra

E None of these

Answer : B

16. Find the synonym of the following word **Perceived**

A anticipated

B unrecognized

C misconceive

D overlook

E None of these

Answer : A

17. Find the synonym of the following word **Agrarian**

A undomesticated

B cultivate

C urban

D metropolitan

E None of these

Answer : A

18. Find the synonym of the following word **Metamorphosis**

A unchanging

B stagnation

C transfiguration

D shrinkage

E None of these

Answer : C

19. Find the synonym of the following word **Amiable**

A aloof

B mean

C unkind

D affable

E None of these

Answer : D

20. Find the synonym of the following word **Dogmatic**

A ambiguous

B stubborn

C submissive

D doubting

E None of these

Answer : B

www.ingramcontent.com/pod-product-compliance
Ingram Content Group UK Ltd.
Pitfield, Milton Keynes, MK11 3LW, UK
UKHW061703190726
13853UKWH00008B/2379